THE NEW TESTAMENT
TESTAMENT
and ETHICS

THE NEW
TESTAMENT
and ETHICS

A BOOK-BY-BOOK SURVEY

EDITED BY

JOEL B. GREEN

B
Baker Academic
a division of Baker Publishing Group
Grand Rapids, Michigan

© 2011, 2013 by Baker Publishing Group

Published by Baker Academic
a division of Baker Publishing Group
P.O. Box 6287, Grand Rapids, MI 49516-6287
www.bakeracademic.com

Printed and bound by CPI Group (UK) Ltd, Croydon, CR0 4YY

The New Testament and Ethics first published in 2013. Chapters for this volume previously appeared in Joel B. Green, ed., Dictionary of Scripture and Ethics (Baker Academic, 2011).

Library of Congress Cataloging-in-Publication Data
The New Testament and ethics : a book-by-book survey / Joel B. Green, editor.
    pages cm
Includes bibliographical references and index.
ISBN 978-0-8010-4936-1 (pbk.)
    1. Ethics in the Bible. 2. Bible. New Testament—Crticism, interpretation, etc. 3. Christian ethics—Biblical teaching. I. Green, Joel B., 1956-
B2545.E8N49 2013
241.5—dc23   2013024423

13   14   15   16   17   18   19   7   6   5   4   3   2   1

CONTENTS

CONTRIBUTORS

Brawley, Robert L. PhD, Princeton Theological Seminary. Professor of New Testament Emeritus, McCormick Theological Seminary.

Chilton, Bruce. PhD, St. John's College, Cambridge University. Bernard Iddings Bell Professor of Religion, Bard College.

Cosgrove, Charles H. PhD, Princeton Theological Seminary. Professor of New Testament Studies and Christian Ethics, Northern Seminary.

deSilva, David A. PhD, Emory University. Trustees' Distinguished Professor of New Testament and Greek, Ashland Theological Seminary.

Donahue, John R., SJ. PhD, University of Chicago. Research Professor in Theology, Loyola University, Maryland.

Downs, David J. PhD, Princeton Theological Seminary. Assistant Professor of New Testament Studies, Fuller Theological Seminary.

Dryden, J. de Waal. PhD, Cambridge University. Associate Professor of Biblical Studies, Covenant College.

Edgar, David Hutchinson. PhD, Trinity College, Dublin. Chester Beatty Library, Dublin.

Furnish, Victor Paul. PhD, Yale University. University Distinguished Professor Emeritus of New Testament, Southern Methodist University.

Green, Joel B. PhD, University of Aberdeen. Professor of New Testament Interpretation, Associate Dean for the Center for Advanced Theological Studies, Fuller Theological Seminary.

Gupta, Nijay K. PhD, University of Durham. Assistant Professor of Biblical Studies, Northeastern Seminary of Roberts Wesleyan College.

Haloviak, Kendra Jo. PhD, The Graduate Theological Union at Berkeley. Assistant Professor of New Testament Studies, La Sierra University.

Horrell, David G. PhD, University of Cambridge. Professor of New Testament Studies, University of Exeter.

Jefford, Clayton N. PhD, The Claremont Graduate School. Professor of Scripture, Saint Meinrad School of Theology.

Ogletree, Thomas W. PhD, Vanderbilt University. Frederick Marquand Professor Emeritus of Ethics and Religious Studies, Yale University Divinity School.

Reese, Ruth Anne. PhD, University of Sheffield. Associate Professor of New Testament, Asbury Theological Seminary.

Simpson, Gary M. ThD, Christ Seminary-Seminex. Professor of Systematic Theology and Director, Center for Missional Leadership, Luther Seminary.

Stassen, Glen H. PhD, Duke University. Lewis B. Smedes Professor of Christian Ethics, Fuller Theological Seminary.

Sumney, Jerry L. PhD, Southern Methodist University. Professor of Biblical Studies, Lexington Theological Seminary.

Verhey, Allen. PhD, Yale University. Professor of Theological Ethics, Duke University Divinity School.

Westmoreland-White, Michael. PhD, The Southern Baptist Theological Seminary. Outreach Coordinator, Every Church a Peace Church.

Wheeler, Sondra E. PhD, Yale University. Carr Professor of Christian Ethics, Wesley Theological Seminary.

ABBREVIATIONS

General

b.	Babylonian Talmud
ca.	circa
chap(s).	chapter(s)
Gk.	Greek
Lat.	Latin
LXX	Septuagint
m.	Mishnah
mg.	margin
NRSV	New Revised Standard Version
NT	New Testament
OT	Old Testament
pars.	parallels
v(v).	verse(s)

Old Testament

Gen.	Genesis
Exod.	Exodus
Lev.	Leviticus
Num.	Numbers
Deut.	Deuteronomy
Josh.	Joshua
Judg.	Judges
Ruth	Ruth
1–2 Sam.	1–2 Samuel
1–2 Kgs.	1–2 Kings
1–2 Chr.	1–2 Chronicles
Ezra	Ezra
Neh.	Nehemiah
Esth.	Esther
Job	Job
Ps./Pss.	Psalms
Prov.	Proverbs
Eccl.	Ecclesiastes
Song	Song of Songs
Isa.	Isaiah
Jer.	Jeremiah
Lam.	Lamentations
Ezek.	Ezekiel
Dan.	Daniel
Hos.	Hosea
Joel	Joel
Amos	Amos
Obad.	Obadiah
Jon.	Jonah
Mic.	Micah
Nah.	Nahum
Hab.	Habakkuk
Zeph.	Zephaniah
Hag.	Haggai
Zech.	Zechariah
Mal.	Malachi

New Testament

Matt.	Matthew
Mark	Mark
Luke	Luke

John	John
Acts	Acts
Rom.	Romans
1–2 Cor.	1–2 Corinthians
Gal.	Galatians
Eph.	Ephesians
Phil.	Philippians
Col.	Colossians
1–2 Thess.	1–2 Thessalonians
1–2 Tim.	1–2 Timothy
Titus	Titus
Phlm.	Philemon
Heb.	Hebrews
Jas.	James
1–2 Pet.	1–2 Peter
1–3 John	1–3 John
Jude	Jude
Rev.	Revelation

Apocrypha and Septuagint

1–4 Macc.	1–4 Maccabees
Sir.	Sirach
Tob.	Tobit
Wis.	Wisdom of Solomon

Old Testament Pseudepigrapha

T. Ash.	Testament of Asher
T. Levi	Testament of Levi
T. Reu.	Testament of Reuben

Dead Sea Scrolls

1QS   Rule of the Community

Rabbinic Tractates

Ber.	Berakot
Šabb.	Šabbat

Other Rabbinic Works

Rab.	Rabbah (+ biblical book)
Sipre	Sipre

Apostolic Fathers

Barn.	Epistle of Barnabas
1–2 Clem.	1–2 Clement
Did.	Didache
Herm. Mand.	Shepherd of Hermes, Mandate(s)
Herm. Sim.	Shepherd of Hermes, Similitude(s)

New Testament Apocrypha and Pseudepigrapha

Apos. Con.	Apostolic Constitutions and Canons

Papyri

P.Bod.   Bodmer Papyri

Greek and Latin Works

Ambrose

Vid.   De viduis

Aristotle

Pol.   Politica

Augustine

Doctr. chr.	De doctrina Christiana (Christian Instruction)
Mor. eccl.	De moribus ecclesiae catholicae (The Way of Life of the Catholic Church)
Serm. dom.	De sermone Domini in monte (Sermon on the Mount)
Virginit.	De sancta virginitate (Holy Virginity)

Cicero

Tusc.	Tusculanae disputationes (Tusculan Disputations)

Clement of Alexandria

Exc. Excerpta ex Theodoto (Excerpts from Theodotus)

Diogenes Laertius

Lives Lives of Eminent Philosophers

Jerome

Epist. Epistulae

Justin Martyr

1 Apol. Apologia i (First Apology)
Dial. Dialogus cum Tryphone (Dialogue with Trypho)

Onasander

Strat. Strategikos (On the Duties of a General)

Origen

Hom. Num. Homiliae in Numeros

Philo

Alleg. Interp. Allegorical Interpretation
Sacrifices On the Sacrifices of Cain and Abel

Plato

Resp. Respublica (Republic)

Pliny the Elder

Nat. Naturalis historia (Natural History)

Plutarch

Cato Maj. Cato Major (Cato the Elder)

Quintilian

Inst. Institutio oratoria

Seneca

Ep. Epistulae morales

Tertullian

Idol. De idololatria (Idolatry)
Ux. Ad uxorem (To His Wife)

Other Authors

John Calvin

Institutes Institutes of the Christian Religion

Thomas Aquinas

ST Summa theologiae

Secondary Sources

AB	Anchor Bible
AGJU	Arbeiten zur Geschichte des antiken Judentums und des Urchristentums
ANTC	Abingdon New Testament Commentaries
ASCE	Annual of the Society of Christian Ethics
ATANT	Abhandlungen zur Theologie des Alten und Neuen Testaments
BECNT	Baker Exegetical Commentary on the New Testament
BETL	Bibliotheca ephemeridum theologicarum lovaniensium
BZNW	Beihefte zur Zeitschrift für die neutestamentliche Wissenschaft
CBQ	Catholic Biblical Quarterly
CC	Continental Commentaries

ExAud	*Ex Auditu*
FCNTECW	Feminist Companion to the New Testament and Early Christian Writings
FRLANT	Forschungen zur Religion und Literatur des Alten und Neuen Testaments
HUT	Hermeneutische Untersuchungen zur Theologie
Int	*Interpretation*
JBL	*Journal of Biblical Literature*
JSNT	*Journal for the Study of the New Testament*
JSNTSup	Journal for the Study of the New Testament: Supplement Series
LNTS	Library of New Testament Studies
MdB	Le monde de la Bible
NICNT	New International Commentary on the New Testament
NovTSup	Supplements to Novum Testamentum
NTL	New Testament Library
NTM	New Testament Monographs
NTR	New Testament Readings
NTT	New Testament Theology
OECS	Oxford Early Christian Studies
RBS	Resources for Biblical Study
RFCC	Religion in the First Christian Centuries
SBLDS	Society of Biblical Literature Dissertation Series
SBLSymS	Society of Biblical Literature Symposium Series
SEC	Studies in Early Christianity
SecCent	*Second Century*
SHCT	Studies in the History of Christian Thought
SHJ	Studying the Historical Jesus
SNTSMS	Society for New Testament Studies Monograph Series
SNTW	Studies in the New Testament and Its World
THNTC	Two Horizons New Testament Commentary
WBC	Word Biblical Commentary
WUNT	Wissenschaftliche Untersuchungen zum Neuen Testament
WW	*Word and World*

INTRODUCTION

Joel B. Green

For a long time, study of the Bible and study of Christian ethics (or moral theology) were regarded as separate enterprises. This is true to such a degree that those of us who want to study the two together, Scripture *and* Christian ethics, face a series of important questions. These questions cannot forestall our work, though, because of the importance of the Old and New Testaments for Christian ethics. The church that turns to the Bible as Christian Scripture does so on account of its belief that the Bible is authoritative for faith and life, for what we believe and what we do. Working out the shape of faithful life before God, then, necessarily involves interacting with, learning from, and sometimes struggling with the church's Scriptures.

Affirming the nonnegotiable relationship of the Bible to faithful life is only the beginning, however. A cascade of issues immediately follows as we seek to flesh out how the Bible might function authoritatively in theology and ethics. Indeed, the church's history serves as a warning in this regard. This is because the Bible has been used to support immorality and injustices of many kinds—for example, the marginalization and abuse of women, the institution of slavery, a constellation of racist practices, and the persecution of the Jewish people. The Bible has been badly used and misappropriated—sometimes scandalously through its being commandeered to serve the aims of those in power and sometimes simply through unskilled reading. In such cases as these, it seems that we need protection from the Bible, or at least from its interpreters. It is easy enough, then, to recognize the importance of raising and addressing some methodological issues.

What questions require our attention? Some are obvious, others more subtle. Among the more pressing would be the following:

- What of the historical rootedness of the biblical materials? These texts come from another time and place, and work with some commonly held assumptions and social realities that we no longer share. Jesus directs his followers to wash each other's feet, for example. Here we find as straightforward a command as Jesus' directive at the Last Supper that his followers eat the bread and drink the cup in his remembrance. Yet most Christian traditions ignore it, or they transform it into an abstract principle, like "serve each other." But why should we convert the practice of foot-washing into an abstraction while making the Lord's Supper central to Christian worship? Expanding our horizons, other questions arise. What of concubinage, household duty codes, or inheritance laws, for example, and other such matters firmly rooted in the ancient soil in which the biblical books were written?
- What of the many, sometimes competing, voices we hear in the Bible? Written over hundreds of years and in response to evolving situations, the biblical materials do not always speak with a common voice on the questions they address. When, if at all, is divorce an allowable option, and for whom? Should we, or should we not, eat meat sacrificed to idols?
- What of the fact that the biblical materials have their ethical concerns, we have ours, and these two do not always coincide? For most us in the West, eating meat sacrificed to idols is not a pressing concern, but it attracted its share of attention from Paul and the writers of Acts and Revelation. Nor do many of us think much about gleaning rights or other forms of economic sharing, even if Old Testament instruction on such practices begs for renewed attention. (Few preachers talk as much about poverty and the poor as the Bible does!) Conversely, the biblical writers could hardly have anticipated the swirl of ethical worries arising from technological advances that today allow us to contemplate and, at least in initial ways, to foster transhumanism. And many of us find ourselves far more concerned than the biblical materials, at least at an explicit level, with environmental ethics.
- What of those biblical texts that seem morally repugnant to us? What are we to make of biblical texts that authorize in God's name the decimation of a people or the stoning of wrongdoers?

To these questions we can add a few others that identify more specifically some methodological conundrums.

- How do we work with and between the Old and New Testaments? Do we give each its own discrete voice? Do we understand the ethics of the

New Testament in continuity with or as a disruption of the moral witness of the Old Testament?

- Do we want to know what the biblical writers *taught* their first readers about faithful life, or do we want to know what the biblical books *teach* us about faithful life? That is, is our task a *descriptive* one, or are we interested in how Scripture might *prescribe* morality?

- Do we learn from the biblical writers the *content* of Christian ethics, or do we learn from them *how to engage in reflection* on Christian ethics? Another way to ask this is to distinguish between what the Old and New Testaments teach about morality and how the Old and New Testament writers go about their ethical reflection. Those whose concern is with the former approach are often interested in setting out the boundaries of appropriate ethical comportment. Those interested in the latter often think that we need to learn from the Bible an approach to ethical reflection that may take us beyond what the biblical materials teach.

- Are we concerned with describing what biblical books teach about right living, or are we concerned with how engagement with the books of the Bible might have the effect of sculpting our character, our dispositions, our commitments, for ethical lives? When we turn to Scripture with a concern for ethics, are we focused first and foremost on "ethics" as moral *decision-making* or as moral *formation*? Do we come to the Scriptures asking, "What should we do?" or do we come asking, "What kind of people ought we to be?"

Undoubtedly, many will want to respond at least to some of the questions with a resounding "both-and" rather than "either-or." Sketching the terms of the conversation like this can help to identify the poles of the discussion, but does not prohibit a range of responses along a continuum.

Even on this sampling of questions, the state of today's discussion about Scripture and ethics supports very little by way of consensus. Naming these issues serves rather to map the terrain, so to speak, or to identify the fault lines in the conversation. Readers of the essays collected here will find that contributors have not been asked to adopt a certain perspective or approach. They have been given the more general task of focusing on the ethics of each of the books of the New Testament and a sampling of subsequent Christian literature, and on the possible significance of each for contemporary Christian ethics. They sketch some of the moral issues explicitly addressed in the book and some of the patterns of moral reasoning displayed in the book. As such, they supplement and extend the conversation begun in the introductory essays on "Ethics in Scripture" and "New Testament Ethics."

Students will find here a needed introduction to the larger conversation concerned with the Bible and ethics, not its final word. Students of the Bible, whether in introductory classes or in more advanced courses concerned with the theology of Scripture, will find a reminder that more is going on with these documents than questions of history or theological debate. Students in Christian ethics will find here an introduction to the ethical witness of the Scriptures, including a reminder of the ways in which moral formation and instruction are always theologically and contextually grounded. A central issue for God's people in every time and place was and remains what it means to be faithful to God in the midst of these challenges, these historical exigencies, these options for faith and life. Whether cast as reflecting the divine image, as loyalty to the covenant, as faithful response to God's liberating initiative, or as imitating Jesus, these texts broadcast as their central concern the identity and ethics of a faithful people. The call to faithful life is not only for people within the biblical stories, or only for the people to whom the biblical materials were first addressed. It remains our call too, and these reflections on the ethical witness of Scripture help to shape the itinerary of the journey ahead.

The essays that follow are selected from the *Dictionary of Scripture and Ethics*, published in 2011 by Baker Academic, and are made available here in order to make them more readily available for use in classroom and personal study. The *Dictionary of Scripture and Ethics* is a major reference tool with over five hundred articles treating not only the biblical books, but a wide array of topics concerned with issues in Christian ethics (like gambling, bioethics, the seven deadly sins, terrorism, and animals) and different approaches to ethics and Scripture (like cross-cultural ethics, Reformed ethics, narrative ethics, Latino/Latina ethics, and virtue ethics). In other words, the conversation begun in the present volume is continued, and expanded, in the dictionary itself.

1

OVERVIEW

♦ Ethics in Scripture ♦

Allen Verhey

Ethics may be defined as disciplined reflection concerning moral conduct and character. In Scripture, such reflection is always disciplined by convictions about God's will and way and by commitments to be faithful to God. Biblical ethics is inalienably theological. To sunder biblical ethics from the convictions about God that surround it and sustain it is to distort it. The fundamental unity of biblical ethics is simply this: there is one God in Scripture, and it is that one God who calls forth the creative reflection and faithful response of those who would be God's people.

That unity, however, is joined to an astonishing diversity. The Bible contains many books and more traditions, each addressed first to a particular community of God's people facing concrete questions of conduct in specific cultural and social contexts. Its reflections on the moral life, moreover, come in diverse modes of discourse. They come sometimes in statute, sometimes in story. They come sometimes in proverb, sometimes in prophetic promises (or threats). They come sometimes in remembering the past, sometimes in envisioning the future. The one God of Scripture assures the unity of biblical ethics, but there is no simple unitive understanding even of that one God or of that one God's will. To force biblical ethics into a timeless and systematic unity is to impoverish it. Still, there is but one God, to whom loyalty is due and to whom God's people respond in all of their responses to changing moral contexts.

Ethics in the New Testament

The one God of creation and covenant, of Abraham and Israel, of Moses and David, of prophet and sage raised the crucified Jesus of Nazareth from the dead. That good news was celebrated among his followers as the vindication of Jesus and his message, as the disclosure of God's power and purpose, and as the guarantee of God's good future. The resurrection was a cause for great joy; it was also the basis for NT ethics and its exhortations to live in memory and in hope, to see moral conduct and character in the light of Jesus' story, and to discern a life and a common life "worthy of the gospel of Christ" (Phil. 1:27).

Jesus and the Gospels

The resurrection was the vindication of Jesus of Nazareth as the Christ. He had come announcing that "the kingdom of God has come near" (Mark 1:15), that the coming cosmic sovereignty of God, the good future of God, was at hand. And he had made that future present; he had made its power felt already in his words of blessing and in his works of healing. He called the people to repent, to form their conduct and character in response to the good news of that coming future. He called his followers to "watch" for it and to pray for it, to welcome its presence, and to form community and character in ways that anticipated that future and responded to the ways that future was already making its power felt in him.

Such was the eschatological shape of Jesus' ethic. He announced the future in axioms such as "Many who are first will be last, and the last will be first" (Mark 10:31; Matt. 19:30; Luke 13:30). He made that future present by his presence among the disciples "as one who serves" (Luke 22:27; cf. Matt. 20:28; Mark 10:45; John 13:2–17). And he called the people to welcome such a future and to follow him in commands such as "Whoever wants to be first must be last of all and servant of all" (Mark 9:35; cf. 10:44). To delight already in a coming kingdom in which the poor are blessed was even now to be carefree about wealth (Matt. 6:25, 31, 34; Luke 12:22) and to give generously to help the poor (Mark 10:21; Luke 12:33). To welcome even now a kingdom that belongs to children (Mark 10:14) was to welcome and to bless them (Mark 9:37). To respond faithfully to a future that was signaled by Jesus' open conversation with women (e.g., Mark 7:24–30; John 4:1–26) was already to treat women as equals. To celebrate God's forgiveness that made its power felt in Jesus' fellowship with sinners (e.g., Mark 2:5; Luke 7:48) was to welcome sinners and to forgive one's enemies.

Because Jesus announced and already unveiled the coming reign of God, he spoke "as one having authority" (Mark 1:22), not simply on the basis of the law or the tradition or the regularities of experience. And because the coming reign of God demanded a response of the whole person and not merely external observance of the law, Jesus consistently made radical demands. So Jesus' radical demand for truthfulness replaced (and fulfilled) legal casuistry about oaths. The radical demand to forgive and to be reconciled set aside (and fulfilled) legal limitations on revenge. The demand to love even enemies put aside legal debates about the meaning of "neighbor." His moral instructions were based neither on the precepts of law nor on the regularities of experience, but he did not discard them either; law and wisdom were qualified and fulfilled in this ethic of response to the future reign of the one God of Scripture.

This Jesus was put to death on a Roman cross, but the resurrection vindicated both Jesus and God's own faithfulness. This one who died in solidarity with the least, with sinners and the oppressed, and with all who suffer was delivered by God. This Jesus, humble in his life, humiliated by religious and political authorities in his death, was exalted by God. When the powers of death and doom had done their damnedest, God raised up this Jesus and established forever the good future he had announced.

The Gospels used the church's memories of Jesus' words and deeds to tell his story faithfully and creatively. So they shaped the character and conduct of the communities that they addressed. Each Gospel provided a distinctive account both of Jesus and of the meaning of discipleship. In Mark, Jesus was the Christ as the one who suffered, and he called for a heroic discipleship. Mark's account of the ministry of Jesus opened with the call to discipleship (1:16–20). The central section of Mark's Gospel, with its three predictions of the passion, made it clear how heroic and dangerous an adventure discipleship could be. "If any want to become my followers, let them deny themselves and take up their cross and follow me" (8:34 [and note the allusions to martyrdom in 8:35; 10:38–39]).

Hard on the heels of that saying Mark set the story of the transfiguration (9:2–8), in which a voice from heaven declared, "This is my Son, the Beloved; listen to him!" It is striking that the voice did not say, "Look at him, all dazzling white." The voice said, "Listen to him." Silent during the transfiguration, Jesus ordered the disciples to say nothing of what they had seen until the resurrection, and then he told them once again that he, the Son of Man, "is to go through many sufferings and be treated with contempt" (9:12). Mark proceeded to tell the story of the passion, the story of a Christ who was rejected, betrayed, denied, deserted, condemned, handed over, mocked, and crucified, but still was the Son of God, the Beloved, and finally vindicated by God. The implications are as clear as they are shocking: Jesus is the Christ not by displaying some tyrannical power, not by lording it over others, but rather by his readiness to suffer for the sake of God's cause in the world and by his readiness to serve others humbly in self-giving love (cf. 10:42–44). And to be his disciple in this world is to share that readiness to suffer for the sake of God's cause and that readiness to serve others humbly in self-giving love.

The call to heroic discipleship was sustained by the call to watchfulness to which it was joined (13:33–37), by the expectation that, in spite of the apparent power of religious leaders and Roman rulers, God's good future was sure to be.

Mark's call to watchful and heroic discipleship touched topics besides the readiness to suffer for the sake of God's cause, and it illumined even the most mundane of them with the same freedom and daring. Discipleship was not to be reduced to obedience to any law or code. Rules about fasting (2:18–22), Sabbath observance (2:23–3:6), and the distinction between "clean" and "unclean" (7:1–23) belonged to the past, not to the community marked by freedom and watchfulness. The final norm was no longer the precepts of Moses, but rather the Lord and his words (8:38). In chapter 10 Mark gathered the words of Jesus concerning marriage and divorce, children, possessions, and political power. The issues were dealt with not on the basis of the law or conventional righteousness, but rather on the basis of the Lord's words, which appealed in turn to God's intention at creation (10:6), the coming kingdom of God (10:14–15), the cost of discipleship (10:21), and identification with Christ (10:39, 43–45). Mark's Gospel provided no moral code, but it did nurture a moral posture at once less rigid and more demanding than any code.

Matthew's Gospel utilized most of Mark, but by subtle changes and significant additions Matthew provided an account of Jesus as the one who fulfills the law, as the one in whom God's covenant promises are fulfilled. And the call to discipleship became a call to a surpassing righteousness.

Matthew, in contrast to Mark, insisted that the law of Moses remained normative. Jesus came not to "abolish" the law but to "fulfill" it (Matt. 5:17). The least commandment ought still to be taught and still to be obeyed (5:18–19; 23:23). Matthew warned against "false prophets" who dismissed the law and sponsored lawlessness (7:15–27). To the controversies about Sabbath observance Matthew added legal arguments to show that Jesus did what was "lawful" (12:1–14; cf. Mark 2:23–3:6). From the controversy about ritual cleanliness Matthew omitted Mark's interpretation that Jesus "declared all foods clean"

(Mark 7:19; cf. Matt. 15:17); evidently, even kosher regulations remained normative. In Matthew's Gospel the law held, and Jesus was its best interpreter (see also 9.9–13, 19.3–12, 22:34–40).

The law, however, was not sufficient. Matthew accused the teachers of the law of being "blind guides" (23:16, 17, 19, 24, 26). They were blind to the real will of God in the law, and their pettifogging legalism hid it. Jesus, however, made God's will known, especially in the Sermon on the Mount. There, he called for a righteousness that "exceeds that of the scribes and Pharisees" (5:20). The Beatitudes (5:3–11) described the character traits that belong to such righteousness. The "antitheses" (5:21–47) contrasted such righteousness to mere external observance of laws that left dispositions of anger, lust, deceit, revenge, and selfishness unchanged. This was no calculating "works-righteousness"; rather, it was a self-forgetting response to Jesus' announcement of the kingdom (4:12–25).

Matthew called the community to play a role in moral discernment and discipline. The church was charged with the task of interpreting the law, vested with the authority to "bind" and "loose" (18:18), to make legal rulings and judgments. These responsibilities for mutual admonition and communal discernment were set in the context of concern for the "little ones" (18:1–14) and forgiveness (18:21–35), and they were to be undertaken with prayer (18:19). Jesus was still among them (18:20), still calling for a surpassing righteousness.

In Luke's Gospel, the emphasis fell on Jesus as the one "anointed . . . to bring good news to the poor" (4:18). Mary's song, the Magnificat (1:46–55), sounded the theme early on as she celebrated God's action on behalf of the humiliated and hungry and poor. In Luke, the infant Jesus was visited in a manger by shepherds, not in a house by magi (2:8–16; cf. Matt. 2:11–12). Again and again—in the Beatitudes and woes (6:20–26), for example, and in numerous parables (e.g., 12:13–21; 14:12–24; 16:19–31)—Jesus proclaimed good news to the poor and announced judgment on the anxious and ungenerous rich. Luke did not legislate in any of this; he gave no social program, but he insisted that a faithful response to this Jesus as the Christ, as the "anointed," included care for the poor and powerless. The story of Zacchaeus (19:1–10), for example, made it clear that to welcome Jesus "gladly" was to do justice and to practice kindness. Luke's story of the early church in Acts celebrated the friendship and the covenant fidelity that were displayed when "everything they owned was held in common" so that "there was not a needy person among them" (Acts 4:32–34; cf. 2:44–45; cf. also Deut. 15). Character and community were, and were to be, fitting to "good news to the poor."

The "poor" included not just those in poverty, but all those who did not count for much by the world's way of counting. The gospel was good news, for example, also for women. By additional stories and sayings (e.g., 1:28–30; 2:36–38; 4:25–27; 7:11–17; 10:38–42; 11:27–28; 13:10–17; 15:8–10; 18:1–8), Luke displayed a Jesus remarkably free from the chauvinism of patriarchal culture. He rejected the reduction of women to their reproductive and domestic roles. Women such as Mary of Bethany, who would learn from Jesus and follow him, were welcomed as equals in the circle of his disciples (10:38–42).

And the gospel was good news to "sinners" too, to those judged unworthy of God's blessing. It was a gospel, after all, of "repentance and the forgiveness of sins" (24:47), and in a series of parables Jesus insisted that there is "joy in heaven over one sinner who repents" (15:7; cf. 15:10, 23–24). That gospel of the forgiveness of sins was to be proclaimed "to all nations" (24:47); it was to be proclaimed even to the gentiles, who surely were counted among the "sinners." That story was told, of course, in Acts, but already early in Luke's Gospel the devout old Simeon recognized in the infant Jesus God's salvation "of all peoples" (2:31; cf., e.g., 3:6). The story of the gentile mission may await Acts, but already in the Gospel it was clear that to welcome this Jesus, this universal savior, was to welcome "sinners." And already in the Gospel it was clear that a faithful response to Jesus meant relations of mutual respect and love between Jew and gentile. In the remarkable story of Jesus' healing of the centurion's servant (7:1–10), the centurion provided a paradigm for gentiles, not despising but loving the Jews, acknowledging that his access to God's salvation was through the Jews; and the Jewish elders provided a model for Jews, not condemning this gentile but instead interceding on his behalf. In Acts 15, the Christian community included the gentiles without requiring that they become Jews; the church was to be an inclusive community, a welcoming community, a community of peaceable difference.

John's Gospel told the story in ways quite different from the Synoptic Gospels, and its account of the moral life was also quite distinctive. It was written that the readers might have "life in [Jesus'] name" (20:31), and that life was inalienably a life formed and informed by love. Christ was the great revelation of God's love for the world (3:16). As the Father loves the Son (e.g., 3:35; 5:20), so the Son loves his own (13:1). As the Son "abides" in the Father's love and does his commandments, so the disciples are to abide in Christ's love (15:9–10) and keep his commandments. And his commandment was simply that they should love one another as he had loved them (15:12; cf. 15:17). This "new commandment" (13:34) was, of course, hardly novel, but it rested now on a new reality: the love of God in Christ and the love of Christ in his own.

That reality was on display in the cross, uniquely and stunningly rendered by John as Christ's "glory." The Son of Man was "lifted up" on the cross (3:14; 12:32–34). His glory did not come after that humiliating death; it was revealed precisely in the self-giving love of the cross. And that glory, the glory of humble service and love, was the glory that Jesus shared with the disciples (17:22). They too were "lifted up" to be servants, exalted in self-giving love.

The commandment in John was to love "one another" (e.g., 15:12) rather than the "neighbor" or the "enemy." John's emphasis surely fell on mutual love, on relations within the community. But an emphasis was not a restriction, and the horizon of God's love was the whole world (3:16). And as God so loved the world that he sent his Son, so Jesus sent his followers "into the world" (17:18; cf. 20:21). The mission of the Father's love seeks a response, an answering love; it seeks mutual love, and where it finds it, there is "life in Christ's name."

Paul and His Gospel

Before the Gospels were written, Paul had addressed pastoral letters to the churches. He always wrote as an apostle (e.g., Rom. 1:1) rather than as a philosopher or a code-maker. And he always wrote to particular communities facing specific problems. In his letters he proclaimed the gospel of the crucified and risen Christ and called for the response of faith and faithfulness.

The proclamation of the gospel was always the announcement that God had acted in Christ's cross and resurrection to end the reign of sin and death and to establish the coming age of God's own cosmic sovereignty. That proclamation was sometimes in the indicative mood and sometimes in the imperative mood. In the indicative mood, Paul described the power of God to provide the eschatological salvation of which the Spirit was the "first fruits" (Rom. 8:23) and the "guarantee" (2 Cor. 5:5). But the present evil age continued; the powers of sin and death still asserted their doomed reign. The imperative mood acknowledged that Christians were still under threat from these powers and called them to hold fast to the salvation given them in Christ. "If we live by the Spirit, let us also be guided by the Spirit" (Gal. 5:25).

Reflection about the moral life was disciplined by the gospel. Paul called the Romans, for example, to exercise a new discernment, not conformed to this present evil age but instead "transformed by the renewing of your minds" (Rom. 12:2). There is no Pauline recipe for such discernment, no checklist or wooden scheme, but certain features of it are clear enough. It involved a new self-understanding, formed by the Spirit and conformed to Christ (e.g., Rom. 6:11; Gal. 2:20). It involved a new perspective on the moral situation, an eschatological perspective, attentive both to the ways in which the power of God was already effective in the world and to the continuing assertiveness of sin and death. It invoked some fundamental values, gifts of the gospel and of the Spirit, notably freedom (e.g., 2 Cor. 3:17; Gal. 5:1) and love (e.g.,

1 Cor. 13; Phil. 1:9). And it involved participation in a community of mutual instruction (e.g., Rom. 15:14). Discernment was not simply a spontaneous intuition granted by the Spirit, nor did it create rules and guidelines *ex nihilo*. Existing moral traditions, whether Jewish or Greek, could be utilized, but they were always to be tested and qualified by the gospel.

This new discernment was brought to bear on a wide range of concrete issues faced by the churches: the relations of Jew and gentile in the churches, slave and free, male and female, rich and poor. Paul's advice was provided not as timeless moral truths but rather as timely applications of the gospel to specific problems in particular contexts.

The Later New Testament

The diversity of ethics in Scripture is only confirmed by other NT writings. The Pastoral Epistles encouraged a "quiet and peaceable life in all godliness and dignity" (1 Tim. 2:2). It was an ethic of moderation and sober good sense, avoiding the enthusiastic foolishness of others who might claim the Pauline tradition, whether ascetic or libertine.

The subtle theological arguments of the book of Hebrews did not exist for their own sake; they supported and sustained this "word of exhortation" (13:22). The theological basis was the covenant that was "new" (8:8, 13; 9:15; 12:24) and "better" (7:22; 8:6), and the fitting response to that covenant was to "give thanks" and to "offer to God an acceptable worship with reverence and awe" (12:28). Such worship, however, was not a matter of cultic observances. It involved "sacrifice," to be sure, and that "continually," but the sacrifice that is pleasing to God is "to do good and to share what you have" (13:15–16). Hebrews 13 collected a variety of moral instructions, including, for example, exhortations to mutual love, hospitality to strangers, consideration for the imprisoned and oppressed, respect for marriage, and freedom from the love of money.

The Letter of James too was a collection of moral instructions, and a somewhat eclectic collection at that. There was no single theme in James, but there was an unmistakable solidarity with the poor (1:9–11; 2:1–7, 15–16; 4:13–5:6) and a consistent concern about the use of that recalcitrant little piece of flesh, the tongue (1:19, 26; 3:1–12; 4:11; 5:9, 12). James contains, of course, the famous polemic against a "faith without works" (2:14–26), and it seems likely that he had in mind a perverted form of Paulinism, but James and Paul perhaps are not so far apart. When James called for an active faith (2:22), readers of Paul might be reminded of Paul's call for a "faith working through love" (Gal. 5:6).

The ethic of 1 Peter was fundamentally a call to live with integrity the identity and community formed in baptism. The "new birth into a living hope through the resurrection of Jesus Christ from the dead" (1:3; cf. 1:23) was a cause for great joy (1:6, 8), but it was also reason to "prepare your minds for action" and to "discipline yourselves" (1:13). In 1 Peter the author made extensive use of what seem to have been moral traditions associated with instructions for baptism (and which are also echoed in other NT texts [see Selwyn]). The mundane duties of this world in which Christians are "aliens and exiles" (2:11) were not disowned, but they were subtly and constantly reformed by being brought into association with the Christian's new moral identity and community.

The Letters of 2 Peter and Jude defended sound doctrine and morality against the heretics who "promise them freedom" (2 Pet. 2:19). In 2 Peter is a carefully wrought catalog of virtues, beginning with "faith," ending with "love," and including in the middle a number of traditional Hellenistic virtues (1:5–8).

The Johannine Epistles, like the Pastoral Epistles and 2 Peter, defended sound doctrine and morality, but these epistles made their defense in ways clearly oriented to the Johannine perspective. To believe in Jesus—in the embodied, crucified Jesus—is to stand under the obligation to love. In Jesus' death on the cross we know what love is (1 John 3:16). And to know that love is to be called to mutual love within the community (e.g., 1 John 2:9–11; 3:11, 14–18, 23; 4:7–12, 16–21; 2 John 5–6).

The book of Revelation, like most other apocalyptic literature, was motivated by a group's experience of alienation and oppression. In the case of Revelation, the churches of Asia Minor suffered the vicious injustice and petty persecution of the Roman emperor. Revelation encouraged and exhorted those churches by constructing a symbolic universe that made intelligible both their faith that Jesus is Lord and their daily experience of injustice and suffering. The rock on which that universe was built was the risen and exalted Christ. He is "the firstborn of the dead, and the ruler of the kings of the earth" (1:5). He is the Lamb that was slain and is worthy "to receive power and wealth and wisdom and might" (5:12). The victory had been won, but there were still sovereignties in conflict. On the one side were God, his Christ, and those who worship them; on the other side were Satan, his regents, the beasts, and "the kings of the earth," and all those who think to find security with them. The bestiality of empire was on display, and it called for "patient endurance" (1:9; 2:2–3, 10, 13, 19; 3:10; 13:10; 14:12).

The conflict is not a cosmic drama that one may watch as if it were some spectator sport; it is an eschatological battle for which one must enlist. Revelation called for courage, not calculation, for watchfulness, not computation. And "patient endurance" was not passivity. To be sure, Christians in this resistance movement against the bestiality of empire did not take up arms to achieve a power like the emperor's. But they resisted. And in their resistance, even in the style of it, they gave testimony to the victory of the Lamb that was slain.

They were to live courageously and faithfully, resisting the pollution of empire, its cult surely and its lie that Caesar is Lord, but also its murder, fornication, sorcery, and idolatry (cf. the vice lists in 21:8; 22:15; see also 9:20–21). They were to be the voice of all creation, until "those who destroy the earth" would be destroyed (11:18), until the Lord makes "all things new" (21:5).

Ethics in Scripture are diverse, not monolithic. Yet, the one God of Scripture still calls in it and through it for a faithful response, still forms and reforms conduct and character and community until they are something "new," something "worthy of the gospel of Christ."

Bibliography

Barton, J. *Ethics and the Old Testament*. 2nd ed. SCM, 2002.

Birch, B. *Let Justice Roll Down: The Old Testament, Ethics, and the Christian Life*. Westminster John Knox, 1991.

Burridge, R. *Imitating Jesus: An Inclusive Approach to New Testament Ethics*. Eerdmans, 2007.

Hays, R. *The Moral Vision of the New Testament: Community, Cross, and New Creation; A Contemporary Introduction to New Testament Ethics*. HarperSanFrancisco, 1996.

Mendenhall, G. *Law and Covenant in Israel and the Ancient Near East*. Biblical Colloquium, 1955.

Selwyn, E. *The First Epistle of St. Peter*. 2nd ed. Macmillan, 1947.

Verhey, A. *Remembering Jesus: Christian Community, Scripture, and the Moral Life*. Eerdmans, 2002.

von Rad, G. *The Problem of the Hexateuch and Other Essays*. Trans. E. Trueman Dicken. Oliver & Boyd, 1966, 1–78.

Wolff, H. "The Kerygma of the Yahwist." Pages 41–66 in W. Brueggemann and H. Wolff, *The Vitality of Old Testament Traditions*. John Knox, 1975.

Wright, C. *Old Testament Ethics for the People of God*. InterVarsity, 2004.

◆ Scripture in Christian Ethics ◆

Charles H. Cosgrove

A History

Throughout the history of the church Christians have looked to the Bible for theological concepts by which to understand their moral obligations, commandments by which to live, values by which to order personal and social existence, patterns of life worthy of emulation, and insight into the dynamics of character formation. At the same time, the Bible has been used along with other sources of moral understanding (acknowledged and unacknowledged) and has been read in a wide variety of cultural contexts that have shaped the way it has been interpreted.

The Early Church

In the NT direct appeal to the Bible in ethical exhortation and instruction is not nearly as frequent as appeal to other authorities. In the Gospels, Jesus is the chief model and authority for ethics. Elsewhere too we find appeals to the example or teaching of "Jesus" or "Christ" or "the Lord Jesus," and so forth (e.g., Rom. 15:1–3; Phil. 2:5–11; Eph. 5:2; 1 Tim. 6:3; 1 Pet. 2:21–23). Other normative voices are civic authorities (Rom. 13:1–5; 1 Pet. 2:13–15); household authorities—masters (Col. 3:22; 1 Pet. 2:18), husbands (Eph. 5:22; Col. 3:18; 1 Pet. 3:1), and parents (Col. 3:20; Eph. 6:1); church leaders (Phlm. 8, 21; Heb. 13:17); common knowledge (Rom. 1:29–32; cf. 1 Cor. 5:1), including knowledge of one's duties (Rom. 13:6–7); and traditional Christian instruction in so-called vice and virtue lists (1 Cor. 6:9–10; Gal. 5:19–23). The Jewish Scriptures figure in ethical argument and exhortation sometimes independently and sometimes in connection with other sources and authorities.

The Mosaic law became a subject of great debate in the early church. Throughout the early period, appeals to Scripture as a rule for ethics were complicated by the fact that an increasingly influential wing of the church rejected the Mosaic law as a norm for the church or defended a complex (and perhaps sometimes confused and uncertain) understanding of its bearing on questions of behavior. For Paul, the law's authority as a rule for righteousness has terminated in Christ (Rom. 3:21–4:25; 10:1–13; Gal. 3:6–4:7). Nevertheless, the ethic of Christ coincides at points with Mosaic commandments; and love, which Christ commands, fulfills the central purpose of the law (Rom. 13:8–10; Gal. 5:13–14). Moreover, since Scripture was written for "us" (those in Christ who live at the end of the age), Paul reads Deut. 25:4 allegorically as a warrant for apostolic rights (1 Cor. 9:8–10) and interprets Ps. 69:9 christologically in describing Jesus' self-giving way as an example to be imitated (Rom. 15:3). Paul also bases instructions about nonretaliation on Deut. 32:35 and Prov. 25:21–22 (see Rom. 12:19–20), and in a few places he adduces cautionary moral examples from Scripture (1 Cor. 10:1–11; 2 Cor. 11:3).

The conviction that love is central to the Mosaic law was already taught by ancient Jewish rabbis. Mark and Luke attribute this belief to Jesus but imply that other Jewish teachers affirmed it as well (Mark 12:28–34; Luke 10:25–28). In Matthew, Jesus teaches that all the law and the prophets "hang" on the two Great Commandments (Matt. 22:40). One can understand Jesus' opinions in controversies over the law as instances of applying the love command as an interpretive rule (e.g., Matt. 12:1–8, 9–13). In the Sermon on the Mount, however, Jesus casts his teaching at several points in the form, "You have heard that it was said [in the law of Moses]. . . . But I say to you . . ." (Matt. 5:21–22, 27–28, 31–32, 33–34, 38–39, 43–44). Is this reinterpretation, which upholds the authority of the law but asserts that Jesus is the authoritative interpreter, or is it supersession of the law's authority, making Jesus the sole authority and rendering the law's specific commandments obsolete? Other parts of Matthew favor the first alternative (see Matt. 5:17–20; 8:4).

Jewish followers of Jesus had already been shaped by their upbringing in the synagogue, where Scripture (especially the Torah or Pentateuch) was central. Hence, much of the moral instruction of the early church takes for granted prevailing Jewish views about various moral subjects, including sexual ethics, concern for the poor, gender roles, the virtues that should characterize a godly person, and so forth. These assumptions occasionally become explicit in appeals to Scripture that rest on traditional Jewish interpretation (e.g., 1 Tim. 2:9–15). The Jewish heritage is especially evident in the most common form of direct moral appeal to Scripture, the example. Paul singles out Abraham as a man of steadfast trust in God (Rom. 4); so does Hebrews, mentioning other exemplary biblical figures as well (Heb. 11). James refers to the prophets and Job as examples of suffering and patience (Jas. 5:10–11). Negative examples are also adduced: Lot's wife (Luke 17:32); Israel (1 Cor. 10:1–11; Heb. 3:16–4:11); disobedient angels, Sodom and Gomorrah, Cain, Balaam, and Korah (Jude 6–11); Esau (Heb. 12:16); and Cain (1 John 3:12).

The Patristic Period

By the second century, the church possessed not only the Jewish Scriptures but also apostolic writings (Gospels, the letters of Paul, etc.) as guides for ethical reflection. On many topics the church fathers worked out views consistent with the ethics of Greek and Roman philosophers by claiming that the Greeks had stolen their ideas from Moses and by articulating a theory of natural law available to all human beings. The concept of natural law came from philosophy, but the fathers found support for the idea in Rom. 1.

The church also staked out distinctive positions on moral questions such as service in the army, abortion and infanticide, and sexuality. Regarding participation in the Roman army, Jesus' "disarming" of Peter in Gethsemane was a crucial prooftext (Matt. 26:52), taken as signaling a new era of nonviolence for God's people that superseded the old era, in which violence was sanctioned by God (Tertullian, *Idol.* 19). The *Didache* and the *Epistle of Barnabas* include abortion in lists of prohibitions modeled on the Ten Commandments (*Did.* 2.2; *Barn.* 19.5). Later church teachers developed this position by working out theories of the embryo as a living person (with a soul), as evidenced by, for example, the fetal kick of John the Baptist (anonymous Christian cited in Clement of Alexandria, *Exc.* 50).

The fathers generally affirmed the Pauline rule of freedom from the Mosaic law but worked out their own understandings of it. By the middle of the second century Christians were distinguishing between commandments meant to be taken literally by the church and commandments meant to be interpreted only spiritually. According to Justin Martyr, some laws have enduring force because they are moral law; some concern the mystery of Christ; some were given because of Israel's hardness of heart and had only a temporary purpose (see Justin Martyr, *Dial.* 44; 46). According to the author of the *Epistle of Barnabas*, the Jews were deceived by an evil angel into interpreting the Mosaic laws of sacrifice and so forth literally (9.4), but Moses wrote "in the Spirit" (10.2, 9) for those who have heard the "voice of the Lord" (9.7) and are spiritually circumcised in their hearing (10.12).

At the same time, Jewish teaching remained an important influence in Christian ethical instruction—for example, in Christian adoption of the "two ways." Developed in Judaism as an interpretation of the two paths set forth in Deut. 30, the "two ways" concept assumed a variety of forms. Christian versions appear in *Did.* 1–5; *Barn.* 18–20; *Apos. Con.* 7. Book 1 of the *Didache* (*Did.* 1.1–6.2) is a paraphrase of teachings known to us from the Sermon on the Mount. Otherwise, the instructions in *Did.* 1–5 and *Barn.* 18–20 contain practically no material drawn directly from the oral Jesus tradition, the Gospels, or other first-century "apostolic" writings (such as the letters of Paul or James). But one can see forms of ethical expression found also in the Sermon on the Mount and the letters of Paul, particularly the vice and virtue list and the apothegm (a succinct moral directive sometimes briefly elaborated). By contrast, Scripture is used heavily in the moral instructions in book 7 of the *Apostolic Constitutions*, where the "two ways" teaching is explicitly traced to Deut. 30:15, the apothegm is the primary form of instruction, and specific apothegms are drawn from many different parts of the Bible.

Hostile attitudes toward Jewish conceptions of God, creation, and the moral life existed in some of the Christian groups who styled themselves "gnostics." At least some gnostics taught that the creator depicted in the Jewish Scriptures is an evil deity whose activity as creator and promulgation of the law through Moses brought human souls into spiritual darkness and servitude. A number of gnostic interpreters apparently regarded the Scriptures as in some sense authoritative and devoted considerable energy to interpreting Genesis, which offered them material for working out their spiritual-theological cosmologies of human origins. Some of this commentary survives in the *Apocryphon of John*, the *Hypostasis of the Archons*, and the *Tripartite Tractate*. It appears that gnostics took a dim view of sexuality and bodily appetites, which perhaps made a rigorous asceticism morally normative in most gnostic circles.

In the wider church, the Jewish Scriptures were studied as a source of moral instruction and a reservoir of moral examples. We see this already in *1 Clement*, which begins with a long moral discourse based on biblical examples of behavior to be imitated and avoided (*1 Clem.* 1–12). In a revealing description of what "preaching" meant in the second-century church, Justin Martyr mentions lengthy readings from "the writings of the prophets or the memoirs of his apostles," after which the "president" exhorts the people to imitate what they have heard (*1 Apol.* 67). In time, Christian schools were formed, which included moral instruction through study of biblical examples. Fourth-century Christian school exercises in "characterization" (*ethopoiia*) taught students to imagine what biblical figures might have said in moments of moral crisis (e.g., what Cain said after he killed Abel [P.Bod. 33] and what Abraham, Sarah, and Isaac said after God commanded Abraham to sacrifice Isaac [P.Bod. 20]). This was preparation for the day when the students, as preachers and teachers, would present biblical stories as compelling moral examples.

In addition to extracting moral examples from Scripture, Christian writers backed up their exhortations with one-sentence scriptural proofs. The purpose of these sentences probably was not so much to prove something as to restate the exhortation in scriptural language and thus give it greater motivational force. The use of short proof sentences from Scripture became a staple of Christian moral discourse for later writers, being used in all aspects of moral appeal. For example, in Basil's *Longer Rules*, Scripture sentences are adduced to reinforce a rule of practice, underscore the consequences of a certain action (as a warning or motivation), stress the requirement of right means to an end, and define appropriate ends.

Allusion and unmarked paraphrase of Paul, the Gospels (and oral Jesus tradition), and other earlier Christian writings are also extremely common in the apostolic and postapostolic fathers, many of whom saturate their discourse with phrases from Scripture. Apparently, it was assumed that the audience would detect most of the borrowing, in which case a high concentration of scriptural phrases gave the impression that the speaker's exhortation and instruction were simply the voice of the Bible, as if no interpretation were going on. In fact, the selection and disposition of the scriptural words as they were knitted together by the speaker's own formulations made for a highly interpretive use of Scripture.

Virtually all of the church fathers engaged in forms of allegorical interpretation, a method of exegesis based on the assumption that Scripture contains hidden (encoded) teaching. This often involved the discovery of instruction about the moral-spiritual journey of the individual soul. For example, commenting on the words "Come to Heshbon, let it be built" in a sermon on Num. 21:27 (*Hom. Num.* 13), Origen interprets "Hesh-bon" as the soul torn and emptied of its pagan beliefs and immoral habits, then rebuilt and outfitted with pious thoughts, correct understanding, and upright morals. As a general rule, the literal sense of the apostolic writings was regarded as the guide and control on allegorical interpretation. Some fathers spoke of a "rule of truth" or "rule of faith" as normative for interpretation (e.g., Irenaeus, Tertullian, Augustine). This rule, which included an ethical aspect, was regarded as expressing the essentials of apostolic teaching.

Some church fathers differentiated between higher and lower forms of Christian moral life. The idea is perhaps suggested already in *Herm. Sim.* 56.3 and *Did.* 6.2 (cf. Tertullian, *Ux.* 1.3). Advocates appealed to what they saw as evidence of such a distinction in the NT, in 1 Cor. 7:25–38; Rom. 3:3 (so Origen); Matt. 19:21 (so Ambrose). Ambrose and Augustine distinguished between "precepts" (mandatory for all) and "counsels" (freely chosen only by some), a distinction that became basic to the thinking of the medieval church (Ambrose, *Vid.* 12.72; 14.82; Augustine, *Virginit.* 15.15).

The fathers also took up specific moral issues, relying on various sources of inquiry in their day. These included, along with Scripture, "common knowledge" based on custom and cultural consensus and arcane knowledge based on specialized inquiry. For example, advocates of an ascetic lifestyle drew on philosophical asceticism, medicine, and Scripture in working out their teachings on fasting, sexual abstinence, and other forms of bodily self-denial. Often appeals to the various authorities were tightly interwoven. For example, Jerome counsels the widow Furia about how to ward off sexual desire by interpreting 1 Cor. 6:18 in the light of Galen's theory that certain foods stoke the body's internal heat, arousing passion (Jerome, *Epist.* 54.9). Similarly, Augustine seems to assume some current medical-philosophical conception of gestation when, commenting on Exod. 21:22, he says that the question of murder does not arise where the fetus is "unformed."

Augustine was the most important figure of the patristic period for the future of Christian theology and ethics in the Western church. He accepted the allegorical method but cautioned against excesses and insisted on respect for the letter. Augustine worked out what we would call an "ethic of interpretation," emphasizing that judgments about which interpretations of the text to embrace should be guided by love of God and neighbor, a view that manifestly reflects Matt. 22:40 (*Doctr. chr.* 1.36.40). Augustine also found a basis in Jesus' teaching for the principle that intent, as consent to an action and not simply desire, is the basic criterion for evaluating moral action. Hence, although adultery is wrong, it might be permissible in certain cases, such as when a wife yields to the sexual advances of a wealthy suitor in order to get money that her husband desperately needs to pay his taxes, provided she does not submit out of desire for the man (*Serm. dom.* 1.16.50).

The Medieval Period

The fathers developed the concept of the inspiration of Scripture by the Holy Spirit, and by the fourth century the basic contours of the canon were established. They also assumed that Scripture contains levels of meaning beyond the ordinary meaning of its words. The fifth-century theologian John Cassian formalized this hermeneutical tradition of multiple senses of Scripture into a fourfold scheme: historical (literal), allegorical (Christ and his church), anagogical (eschatological/heavenly), and tropological (having to do with the moral-spiritual formation of the soul). Thus, a number of fundamental interpretative assumptions were established in the early centuries of the church and taken over by the medieval church. To illustrate, in the Latin-speaking West the author (Lat. *auctor*) of Scripture was identified as the Holy Spirit and distinguished from the writer (Lat. *scriptor*) of a book of Scripture, the writer being a human being whom the Spirit used as an instrument. The concept of the unified authorship of Scripture justified interpreting passages far apart in time and place in the light of one another. Moreover, almost everyone assumed that Scripture contains secrets veiled under shadow and figure that could be discovered through allegorical interpretation. The plain sense set a certain limit on what allegorical exegesis could discover, but the latter also offered a way to find cherished philosophical concepts in biblical books that looked unphilosophical at the literal level. Greek moral philosophy, which focused on the formation of character, had been an influential conversation partner of the fathers. In the medieval period the allegorical method helped build a conceptual bridge between the unified authorship of Scripture and the newly rediscovered *Nicomachean Ethics* of "the Philosopher" (Aristotle).

The relation of Scripture to the world was also conceived differently than in the days when the church's relation to the world was essentially opposi-tional—as in early Christian apocalyptic but also in the pre-Constantinian church's sense of being an alien minority in a hostile world from which the path to martyrdom or the way of monastic and ascetic life was the noblest means of resistance and escape. The growth of the church in the fourth cen-tury and the changed political situation prompted a reconceptualization that affected how Scripture was read "historically" and "politically" in the early medieval period. In several works Eusebius had already woven scriptural history together with pagan history to form a salvation-historical narrative in which the Jewish patriarchs were cast as superior in understanding to their pagan counterparts. The Christian poet Prudentius viewed not only the Jewish but also the pagan past as preparatory (in a typological way) for the revelation in Christ and as part of a unified salvation history. Working in a similar vein, later minds not only read wider history in the light of Scripture but also interpreted Scripture in the light of wider history. Hence, in 492, responding to a crisis in which the current emperor claimed authority over the church in doctrinal matters, Pope Gelasius I argued that the emperors of Rome ceased to exercise priestly authority once Christ appeared, showing that Christ, the true priest and king, had in effect established a new relation between priestly and royal power. Apparently, Gelasius treated history and Scripture as both divinely authored, with Scripture providing clues to the meaning of history and history providing clues to the meaning of Scripture.

The new view of Christ's relation to temporal power encouraged the use of the OT for models of rulership (kingship), but the relation between church and state had to be worked out. Gelasius observed that in the past some persons, such as Melchizedek, were both kings and priests, but that when Christ ap-peared, the true king and priest (an allusion to the Christology of Hebrews), he established a separation of these offices. In the twelfth century, the convic-tion that Christ is the true and supreme king over the world inspired the idea that the pope is the vicar (representative) of Christ. This meant that whatever Scripture says of Christ could be applied to the pope as his vicar. Allegorical interpretation of the "two swords" text in Luke 22:38 proved that the priesthood possesses both spiritual and political authority. Hence, it became plausible to use OT stories of kings, along with other passages deemed to speak (literally or allegorically) about temporal power, in support of a pontiff's political aims and actions. Notable examples of this kind of self-serving exegesis are found in the "political" sermons of Pope Clement VI (1291–1352).

The Christ of the Gospels was also the model for the Christian life gener-ally. Naturally, the proper way to imitate Christ was debated. One of the most pronounced discussions concerned the poverty of Christ. This interpretive conflict reached particular intensity in the fourteenth century between the Franciscans, who insisted that imitation required a vow of absolute poverty, and Pope John XXII, who rejected the claim that Jesus had ever embraced absolute poverty. Both sides appealed to a common fund of biblical passages. Central was how to understand the instructions in Matt. 10:9–10 to the disciples, when they are sent out on their mission, about taking no gold, silver, copper, and so on, a topic that led to the question of whether Pope John XXII had violated a "natural right" when he legally annulled Franciscan poverty in a series of bulls in 1322–23. William of Ockham's defense of the Franciscans helped to establish the concept of a natural right as a freedom, a notion that would outlive the debate about Christ's poverty.

In the medieval world, rules for the ordering of life under churchly authority, including moral behavior and discipline, were developed in what came to be known as "canon law," a loose body of authoritative tradition that was eventually systematized in the twelfth and thirteenth centuries in Gratian's *Decretum* and a collection of papal decretals assembled by Raymond of Peñafort under Pope Gregory IX. Sources included the Bible and Roman law as well as papal and conciliar decrees. In this era, but less so in subsequent development of canon law, the influence of the Bible was conspicuous. According to Gratian, the Bible reveals natural law, which is distinct from human custom, and in his *Decretum* the Bible figures prominently as a source of prooftexts.

The work of codifying and interpreting canon law differed from moral theology, the primary purpose of which was not to articulate and interpret rules but rather to give an intelligible account of the moral-spiritual formation of the soul in preparation for heaven and the beatific vision. This went back to Augustine, who also inherited from his Christian and pagan predecessors a view of ethics as virtue-centered and oriented to character formation. Hence, the great French scholastic Peter Abelard (1079–1142) opened his treatise on ethics (*Scito te ipsum*) with the statement "We regard morals as the virtues and vices of the mind that make us prone to good or bad deeds."

In the theological *summa* (a systematic compendium of theology), discussion of right action assumed the teaching of the church (codified in various bodies of canon law), which the scholars sought to interpret, not debate. The scholastics applied reason to moral questions in the light of Scripture and through interaction with other revered authorities—the church fathers and certain ancient philosophers regarded as sources of insight, to be reconciled where possible, not simply as debate partners.

Byzantine scholars transmitted ancient commentaries on Aristotle's *Nicomachean Ethics* and wrote their own commentaries on the same. The Byzantine interest in Greek philosophical ethics is also evinced in a Christianized version of Epictetus's *Enchiridion*, which served as a cherished introduction to ethics in the East, and Eastern moral exegesis of Scripture appeared in all kinds of works, including ascetical writings on prayer and spirituality. Nevertheless, Eastern Christian ethics did not become the subject of treatises but rather was treated almost exclusively as a dimension of theology, specifically, as a basic aspect of divine communion (or "deification").

The importance of the ancient Greek philosophical tradition for Western medieval scholars led to debates about whether philosophy (and philosophical ethics) could be legitimately pursued on its own terms as an inquiry separate from theological ethics and the revelation in Scripture. One advocate of this conceptual separation was Albert the Great, who wrote the first Latin commentary on the whole of Aristotle's *Nicomachean Ethics*. In conversation with Aristotle, Albert defined happiness as intellectual contemplation of immaterial, invisible realities achieved through detachment from earthly things through ascent to the divine. In his commentaries on the *Nicomachean Ethics*, Albert quoted Scripture only rarely. For example, in his extensive treatment of chapter 10 in his first commentary on the *Nicomachean Ethics*, Albert quotes Scripture only about ten times. Far more frequent are quotations from the fathers and from more recent scholars (including other commentators on Aristotle). The relative absence of Scripture owes in part to the topics, which often do not lend themselves to easy prooftexting from Scripture, and above all to the nature of the discourse as Albert conceives it: a philosophical discussion based on reason with only minimal recourse to proofs from the Bible. This approach was typical of a good deal of philosophically oriented medieval discussions of ethics. Methodologically, philosophical ethics, unlike theological ethics, did not rely on Scripture and Christian tradition but rather was conducted on the basis of reason through commentary on classical philosophers such as Aristotle. Hence, the commentary on the *Nicomachean Ethics* by the great thirteenth-century philosopher and theologian Thomas Aquinas (*Sententia libri ethicorum*) does not refer to Scripture at all.

Scripture does play a role in Thomas Aquinas's *Summa theologiae*, including the second part, where he examines the conditions of moral existence and its philosophical foundations. Thomas begins with the purpose of human life and the nature of the moral life (human action, passions and habits, vice and virtue, law and grace), then goes on to examine specific virtues and vices. These include the primary "theological" (or "supernatural") virtues of faith, hope, and charity, along with the chief "natural" virtues of prudence, justice, fortitude, and temperance. Conceiving moral existence in terms of virtues and vices was a traditional approach, going back to the fathers and especially to Augustine, who derived the theological virtues from Scripture (with 1 Cor. 13:13 providing the hermeneutical key) and the natural virtues from the Greco-Roman philosophical tradition as mediated through Christian reflection.

The sections of Thomas's *Summa theologiae* dealing with ethics take the same form as other parts of the work. He presents logical analyses set forth in a consistent pattern of formal disputation (proposition, objections to it, his answer, and his replies to the objections) in which authorities are quoted from time to time. These authorities are Scripture, church fathers (Augustine, Ambrose, and others), certain ancient philosophers (especially Aristotle), and occasionally another source such as canon law. One or more of these authorities may be found in many arguments, but not every argument contains an appeal to authority. Quotations from Scripture appear in some objections, but most are found in Thomas's statement of his own view (in contraries, answers, and replies). These quotations are almost always a single sentence from the Bible: a declaration, often in the form of a *sententia* (apothegm) or treated as such; a statement about what God does (past, present, or future tense); or an exhortation that can be treated as expressive of a principle or as showing a relation between concepts. The scriptural sentences are used in various ways: as a major premise in an argument, as a supplemental proof of a conclusion of an argument, as a formulation of a contrary, as evidence for the meaning of a key word or concept, and as a basis for drawing an inference about a relation between concepts. Thomas rarely appeals to anything but the plain sense of Scripture, although he does not oppose the hermeneutic of multiple senses and argues that the ceremonial and judicial laws of the OT have figurative meanings. He also never debates the interpretation of a text but almost always treats the meaning of Scripture as self-evident; only very occasionally does he cite an authority for an interpretation of Scripture (e.g., *ST* II-I, q. 4, a. 2).

A different rhetorical form of ethical discourse is found in Abelard's *Scito te ipsum*, a logical-philosophical analysis of moral culpability in which Scripture figures not only as a fund of *sententiae* but also as a source of moral examples. Sometimes Abelard expounds the meaning of a scriptural sentence. He also sometimes brings together groups of scriptural statements and discusses their interrelation as he develops a point, always assuming the inherent unity of Scripture. It is apparent that Scripture profoundly shaped Abelard's thinking. At the same time, he depended on the scholastic tradition for concepts and questions for interpreting Scripture.

A common theme in scholastic ethics is the nature of love as the central moral teaching of the Bible. The NT and the fathers bequeathed to the later church the conviction that love is the highest affection and the supreme virtue. Augustine, on whom medieval thinkers heavily depended, sought to encapsulate this teaching in an epigram: "Love, and do what you will" (*Tract. ep. Jo. 7.8*). For Augustine, love was not simply a criterion for judging right from wrong but rather a "weight" in the heart that moves the will to a good purpose and ultimately to union with God (*Conf.* 13.9.10). In this sense, love is passional but in a spiritual sense, without bodily desire.

The idea that love, rightly understood, lacks sexual desire might have posed problems for the medieval efforts to interpret Song of Songs, but ever since Origen, that book had been interpreted as an allegory of spiritual love: Christ the bridegroom burning with celestial love for the church (or for the soul of each believer). Origen called that love *eros* (much less frequently *agape*) and thus inspired a spiritual eroticism of commentary on Song of Songs. Medieval divines interpreted Song of Songs on the basis of the fourfold reading of Scripture, which included a tropological (moral) sense. The tropological *modus* was variously understood as speaking in Song of Songs of the nuptials of the soul and Christ in a purifying spiritual ascent (Honorius); the soul's progression through faith, hope, and charity (Bernard of Clairvaux); the soul as a bride whom the Spirit makes "fertile with the offspring of the virtues" (the *Eulogium sponsi di sponsa* [PL 176, 987C]); and so forth. The medieval tradition of commentary on Song of Songs also saw a shift from expositions focused on the higher moral-spiritual life of the cloistered to interpretations that applied Song of Songs to the more general human struggle to order and direct desire.

The book of Psalms also offered expressions of the soul's ardent love for God and was revered as an innerbiblical corpus containing virtually everything found elsewhere in Scripture. That comprehensiveness was understood as including a moral voice in which David's colloquy with God is also David's dialogue with the church. David was seen as both a moral exemplar and a moral instructor. In commentary and preaching, as well as paraphrases and imitations of the psalms, David was taught as a model of compunction and penance, a source of soothing words to the soul in spiritual pain, and an example of justifiable individual and collective complaint in the midst of spiritual and temporal sufferings. Richard Rolle (1290–1349) extolled the psalms as medicine for the sick soul, urging recitation of them as a means to attain a vision of heaven. An instance of politically charged use of the complaint psalms is John Lydgate's rewriting of Ps. 136 in his *Defense of Holy Church* (1413–14). Lydgate encouraged readers to think of Henry V as a modern-day David who ought to remain vigilant against the political machinations of the Lollards.

The Reformation Era

The various branches of the Protestant Reformation championed the principle of *sola scriptura* and tended to be biblicistic in their approaches to theology and ethics. This biblicism led to reconceptualizations of the relation of church and society. Martin Luther's insistence that gospel and law are fundamentally different revived the old question of how Christians are to understand and make use of the Mosaic law. Reformers who represented what came to be known as the Lutheran and Reformed branches of Protestantism worked out a threefold use of the law: the law given to constrain behavior (the "first" or "civil" use); the law as God's means of convicting sinners and driving them to the mercy of the gospel (the "second" or "evangelical" use); and the law (or certain parts of law, the Ten Commandments above all) as moral law for the church (the "third" use). The third use of the law first appears in the writings of Philip Melanchthon. Luther seems generally to have affirmed it, although he did not emphasize or expound it. The third use became enshrined as an expression of Lutheran faith in article 6 of the *Formula of Concord* (1577) and was also embraced by John Calvin (*Institutes* 2.7.12), becoming a hallmark of Reformed theology.

Calvin's understanding of the third use of the law was closely connected with his conception of sanctification as a process of increasing conformity to the Ten Commandments. Calvin regarded the Ten Commandments as the most comprehensive revelation of moral principles in Scripture. Under their broad injunctions one could order all the more specific moral instructions of the Bible. Other Reformers gave pride of place to the Sermon on the Mount as the epitome of scriptural ethics, and everyone found a hermeneutical key in Jesus' teaching that all of Scripture "hangs" on the two Great Commandments, love of God and neighbor (Matt. 22:40). For Calvin, the double love command ought to guide the interpretation of individual commandments. For Luther, the double love command showed above all the unity of the law in love as a principle for distinguishing law and gospel.

Another area of fresh discussion was the Sermon on the Mount. Against tradition, Luther argued that this sermon presents not counsels of perfection for the few but rather a gospel ethic to which every Christian is to aspire. At the same time, the sermon defines the moral life of the kingdom of God, not the kingdom of this world—that is, not the social order, which must be governed by law and not by the gospel. The distinction between law and gospel and the doctrine of two kingdoms guided Luther's interpretation of Paul's teaching about civil authority in Rom. 13. According to Luther, the word *person* (*anima* or "soul" in the Vulgate) in Paul's instruction "Let every person be subject to the governing authorities" (Rom. 13:1) includes the pope. Hence, the church does not stand above civil authority and must be obedient to it, at least in matters pertaining to worldly order (*To the Christian Nobility*).

Where Luther sharply distinguished temporal and spiritual authority as belonging to different spheres (different "kingdoms"), other Reformers assumed a greater unity between the two. Of particular significance is Huldrych Zwingli's notion that the ordination of civil authority, according to Rom. 13:1–7, includes the idea, or at least the possibility, that the Christian magistrate who hears the gospel will carry out his office according to God's will (*On Divine and Human Justice*). The concept of the Christian magistrate was a basic hermeneutical axiom in Zwingli's approach to civil authority, and he tended to think of the body of Christ (the *corpus Christianum*) as a unity entailing the whole of society. Accordingly, in his commentary on Jeremiah (1531), Zwingli proposed that when citizens and magistrate heed the gospel, "the Christian city is nothing other than the Christian church." Zwingli interpreted Matt. 18:15–20 (on dealing with an offender) as a basis for the Christian magistrate to exercise the right of excommunication, and he appealed to the fact that the OT spoke of rulers as "shepherds" to argue that the magistrate has a role in church discipline.

If Paul's teaching about law and gospel in Romans and Galatians became guiding canons for Luther and his followers, the concept of discipleship in the Gospels provided the hermeneutical key for the Anabaptists, who made up the bulk of the so-called radical wing of the Reformation. According to Anabaptists, the prescriptions of the Sermon on the Mount are not individual and aspirational goals but rather are divine commands for a disciplined ordering of community life. The Anabaptists stressed the moral transformation of the believer and rejected or downplayed the concept of original sin, emphasizing the teaching in Ezekiel that sons do not inherit the guilt of their fathers (Ezek. 18:4, 20). Christ, they said, makes believers ethically righteous, which is the main point of the only Anabaptist writing that directly discusses "atonement theory" (*On the Satisfaction of Christ* [c. 1530]). The Anabaptist focus on the example and teachings of Jesus as the template for community ethics led most Anabaptists to embrace pacifism (e.g., those influenced by Conrad Grebel and Menno Simons, but not Thomas Müntzer and his followers). Article 6 of the Schleitheim Articles of the Swiss Brethren (1527) summarizes the scriptural basis for nonviolence; almost all the prooftexts come from the example and teaching of Jesus. Moreover, on the basis of Jesus' teaching about discipleship (Matt. 6:19–34; Luke 12:33; 14:33) and descriptions of the community of goods in Acts 2:44–45; 4:32–5:11, Anabaptists also renounced private property (so the Hutterites and Swiss Anabaptists according to the Swiss *Congregational*

Order of 1527) or at least put special importance on simplicity of life and care for the poor. Anabaptists understood the reference in Luke 4:18 to preaching good news to the poor as a crucial expression of the gospel, calling for a church of and for the poor. They also rejected the taking of oaths (on the basis of Matt. 5:33–37).

The Roman response to the Protestant Reformation involved the so-called Counter-Reformation, in which the Council of Trent (1545–64) played a crucial role. At this council the Roman Catholic Church reaffirmed but also revised its canon law, declared that both the Bible and unwritten traditions passed down from the apostles are to be revered as sources of truth, and stressed that the church must be regarded as superior in its judgments over private interpretation (*Decree Concerning the Canonical Scriptures*, Session IV [1546]). But responding to Protestant challenges was not the only concern of the Roman Catholic Church in the sixteenth century. A number of creative thinkers were working on their own questions in the domains of both theology and ethics. A subject bearing on biblical interpretation was "probabilism." Dominican theologian Bartholomew Medina, commenting on Thomas Aquinas, had formulated the following principle: "If an opinion is probable, it may be followed, even if the opposing opinion is more probable" (*Commentary on the Summa* I-II, 19.6). This view became a dominant topic of discussion among sixteenth- and seventeenth-century Roman Catholic divines. In matters of ethics probabilism touched individual moral freedom, and in *Apologema pro antiquissima et universalissima doctrina de probabilitate* (1663), Juan Caramuel analyzed examples of moral action in Scripture in an effort to show that an incipient probabilism is present in Scripture's judgment on those actions.

The Modern (and Postmodern) Era

By the late nineteenth century, questions of personal morality, domestic relations, contemporary social and political problems, the relation of church and state, the duties of citizenship, relations between nations, the proper role of government, the nature of justice, movements such as communism and socialism, questions of human rights, the poor, and so forth were ordered under a discipline of "Christian ethics" (in the Protestant world) or "moral theology" (in Roman Catholicism) distinct from the disciplines of biblical theology and dogmatic theology. This development was an eventual result from a momentous shift in the late eighteenth century when study of the Bible (in the universities of Europe) began to be separated from dogmatic theology as a distinct historical subject. According to the new conception, set forth programmatically by Johann Philipp Gabler in a famous address in 1787, specialists in biblical studies were to supply the theologians with critically established historical descriptions of biblical theology; the theologians, for their part, had the constructive task of translating biblical theology into contemporary thought forms. For Christian ethics, this meant applying the Bible to the questions of the day with awareness of the need for translation from the ancient world into the modern. Christian ethics and moral theology emerged as later disciplinary divisions. In practice, however, no strict division of labor was followed by individual scholars; one finds systematic treatments of ethics that depend on ethicists' and dogmaticians' own interpretations of Scripture, as well as historical studies of biblical ethics that are oriented to modern questions and concerns.

Nevertheless, there was growing agreement that while the Bible has a fixed sense (its historical sense), Christian ethics is a constructive discipline that must constantly evolve to grapple with new issues and to rethink old issues under changed conditions. At the same time, there was an increasing sense of a gap between the diverse moralities of Scripture and what seemed morally proper and rational to the modern mind. This posed a challenge to the Protestant project of basing theology and ethics directly on Scripture. Hence, for some, the Bible's perceived moral deficiencies called for defense through rational interpretation and explanation (e.g., J. A. Hessey, *Moral Difficulties Connected with the Bible* [1871]; Newman Smyth, *The Morality of the Old Testament* [1886]).

The new relation between biblical morality and contemporary moral thought was worked out in terms of new modes of inquiry set in motion by the Enlightenment, which solidified the Cartesian method of inquiry not only in science but also, in modified form, in other fields. In a way that almost defies historical analysis (because of the interaction over centuries of so many political and intellectual forces), the Bible helped create the conditions for the Enlightenment but also became an object of Enlightenment criticism, including criticism based on Enlightenment notions of religion. Advocates of the Enlightenment approach to knowledge championed reason against the authority of institutions (notably the church) and ancient books (the Bible and Aristotle). The recognition by seventeenth-century scientists (*philosophes*) that neither ancient philosophy nor Scripture offered adequate or accurate foundations for inquiries into cosmology, geography, geology, physical anthropology, and the like had led to a distinction between the scope (*scopus*) of philosophy (science) and the scope of Scripture. The province of science was empirical truth; the province of the Bible was the truth about God and salvation. In the eighteenth century this view was increasingly embraced by divines, including John Wesley. They regarded the Bible as authoritative for matters of faith and the moral life, not for knowledge about the physical world.

For some, however, the authority of the Bible was no longer absolute even for doctrine or ethics. Alexander Geddes (1737–1802), an early historical critic, concluded that the divine command that the Israelites exterminate the Canaanites (Josh. 1–3) was not really from God but rather was an invention of "some posterior Jew" (*The Holy Bible*, vol. 2 [1797], ii). This form of moral criticism of Scripture differed from the traditional view going back to the church fathers, who claimed that God had accommodated to "Jewish weakness" by encoding with allegory various practices commanded in the Jewish Scriptures that were later superseded in their literal sense by Christ. Geddes and other Enlightenment Christians treated the Bible like any other ancient book, subjecting it to the same moral criticism that they applied to Homer and other ancient writers. Geddes and other practitioners of what was called "higher criticism" also tended to differentiate the teachings of the OT from the "pure religion of Jesus," which they understood as essentially moral and rational (devoid of the supernatural and of traditional dogma). Intense interest in reconstructing the true history and true religion of Jesus behind the trappings of the Gospels led to numerous portraits of Jesus from 1750 through the early twentieth century, many of which cast Jesus chiefly as an enlightened moral teacher (so Joseph Priestley, G. W. F. Hegel, Ernst Renan, and Adolf von Harnack). The religio-moral authority of Jesus was largely taken for granted in these reconstructions, but the Bible was treated not as an authority but rather as a fallible historical source for recovering the life and teaching of Jesus. This shift from the assumption that authority resides in a text (Scripture) to the view that authority resides in history (in the Jesus of history or in God's activity in history) was one aspect of a broader theological problem posed by the Enlightenment: how could faith rest on the "accidents" of history and the uncertainties of historical knowledge?

For the majority of Christians who continued to accept the authority of Scripture, a number of ethical issues came to the fore as matters of intense debate in the nineteenth century. These included the question of whether the Bible supports slavery (a debate begun by abolitionists who began marshaling Scripture against defenders of the institution) and whether it teaches the subordination of women (to their husbands and to men in general). In working out their arguments from Scripture, women such as Elizabeth Wordsworth, Harriet Beecher Stowe, and Florence Nightingale used the concept of "progressive revelation" (developed by Enlightenment thinkers such as Gotthold Ephraim Lessing) to assign patriarchy (and other things in the OT that they found morally repugnant) to the primitive beginnings of biblical morality.

Moreover, by assuming that the revelation of morality in Scripture is from the primitive to the more enlightened, they plotted an evolutionary trajectory that pointed beyond the limited egalitarian vision of the apostles (such as Paul) to perfect equality of the sexes as God's ultimate will.

The concept of progressive revelation in biblical morality was also embraced by abolitionists such as Francis Wayland to argue that the slaveholding of the patriarchs has less revelatory weight than NT teaching (notably the command of Jesus to love one's neighbor as oneself). Wayland and other abolitionists also developed a hermeneutic of "ethical implication," which seems to have owed something to principles of legal interpretation invoked in nineteenth-century debates about the US Constitution. They argued that the moral teaching of Scripture consists in what is commanded or prohibited in Scripture but also in what is required by or consistent with Scripture's explicit injunctions. Accordingly, they maintained that the system of slavery in America, because it did not recognize the parental rights of slaves, violated implicit ordinances of Scripture, namely, the duty of children to obey parents and of parents to care for and exercise authority over their children (Wayland, *Elements of Moral Science* [1856 edition]).

A good deal of nineteenth-century Protestant ethics entailed establishing Christian morality on the basis of theological doctrines and, with the aid of theophilosophical principles, working out positions on specific moral questions (e.g., in the influential works of Hans Martensen, G. C. A. Harless, and Isaak Dorner). Gabler's program assumed the existence of "universal concepts" by which to translate biblical theology into dogmatic theology. This idea appears to have controlled the constructive efforts of many nineteenth-century Christian ethicists who referred to the Bible only occasionally (and usually in the old prooftexting style of the medieval theologians that they claimed to have superseded) by referring generally to what Scripture "teaches." Thus, it is with breezy confidence that R. F. Weidner asserted (in an epitome of the Christian ethics of Martensen and Harless) that "the education of man for the Kingdom of God" is a basic teaching of Scripture about "the aim of history" (*Christian Ethics*, 2nd ed. [1897], 37). This and similar theophilosophical conceptions of the message of the Bible reflected an age devoted to the idea that history is evolving progressively through increasing enlightenment toward the earthly kingdom of God.

The end of the nineteenth century also saw the birth of the history-of-religions school, which put in question the presumed uniqueness of Israelite and early Christian religion in their ancient religious environments. Within the diverse theological movement known as neoorthodoxy, higher criticism's historical relativization of biblical ethics was met with different responses. For

Rudolf Bultmann, who maintained that there is nothing in the ethics of the NT that an upstanding pagan would not have endorsed, the witness of the gospel, preserved most clearly in Paul, entails freedom not simply from the Mosaic law but from every human convention and moral norm. The Bible bears on ethics not by providing its material criteria but rather by disclosing a way of being characterized by radical faith, which Bultmann expounded through a Christian form of existentialism. Most neoorthodox theologians accepted the results of historical criticism and recognized that the moral teachings of the Bible are diverse, reflecting a variety of practices in different times and places and showing the influence of the beliefs of other ancient Mediterranean peoples. Hence, except within emergent fundamentalism, it was generally agreed that biblical morality had to be mediated through some kind of critical hermeneutic and could not be accepted naively.

In the twentieth century, the use of the Bible in ethics often entailed the assumption that Scripture speaks appropriately to the present not at its moral rule level (the level of specific prescriptions) but only at the level of its general ethical concepts—love, justice, mercy, peace, nonviolence, reconciliation, equality, and so forth (e.g., Paul Ramsey). Some who operated with this hermeneutical assumption attended to biblical rules (commandments and other moral instructions) by looking to the purpose behind the rule and treated that purpose as more important than the letter of the rule.

In addition to taking seriously the problem of the great cultural distance between the social worlds presupposed by biblical morality(ies) and those of the modern era, twentieth-century interpreters also approached biblical ethics with awareness of the apocalyptic assumptions under which NT writers framed their moral instructions. Many interpreters concluded that since the early Christians expected a near end of the world, their instructions about how to live ought to be understood as "interim ethics"—that is, an ethics for the time between the passing present order and the soon-to-arrive new creation. This concept was famously applied to the Sermon on the Mount by Albert Schweitzer but also influenced how Paul's practical instructions to his churches were viewed. Seeing NT ethics as largely interim ethics was another argument against appropriating its teachings at the rule level.

Some twentieth-century interpreters embraced the concept of eschatological transition (found in, e.g., 1 Cor. 7:29–31) and made it the basis of a "crisis ethic." Eschewing moral rules as alien to the gospel, they maintained that every believer is always living between the times and must discover God's will in the crisis created by the tension between the ever-present old and new. Bultmann worked out a crisis ethic through conversation with existentialist philosophy. Karl Barth maintained that ultimately the Christian is called to be obedient not to Scripture but rather to God's personal address, contending that the Bible's witness to God's revelation in Christ prepares one to hear God's command, but that the command is not found in Scripture and must be heard in the concrete situation. Others who adopted the eschatological framework maintained that believers are called to live between the times by embodying the radical ethic of Jesus. The church has to discern the way, but that discernment ought to hew closely to the specific patterns of life expressed in the teachings of the Sermon on the Mount and displayed in the paradigm of Jesus' life (so Stanley Hauerwas).

The scope and the purpose of Christian ethics also were in dispute. In the first half of the century it was largely assumed that, in addition to working out norms for personal ethics, the church has a responsibility to apply Christian ethical principles to society, a task requiring judgments about the bearing of biblical teaching on social and political questions. Advocates of "Christian realism" distinguished the personal from the social, arguing, for example, that the Sermon on the Mount presents an ideal suited to individual moral aspiration but impractical for social life. Social existence requires a realistic ethic of justice worked out in terms of broad biblical concepts, not concrete biblical prescriptions (so Reinhold Niebuhr). In the latter part of the twentieth century a number of influential voices began insisting that the church, not the individual or society, is the proper subject of Christian ethics. The church is called to be a distinct moral community that bears witness to the world by embodying the way of Jesus. The teachings of the Sermon on the Mount and other rigorous NT moral instruction were meant not as a general social ethic or a merely personal ethic but rather as an ethic for the church. For some, this understanding of ecclesial ethics was a way of rejecting the assumptions of Christendom (the notion of a unified Christian social order) in favor of the agonistic relation between the church and the world assumed by the NT (so John Howard Yoder, Stanley Hauerwas). Increasing religious pluralism and secularization made this way of thinking attractive for those who wished to conform their lives in Christian community as closely as possible to what they understood as NT patterns of faith and life without imagining that the church could or should shape the wider society in the image of the kingdom of God.

In Roman Catholic circles natural-law ethics tended to dominate, although after Vatican II there was greater interest in a renewal of moral theology nourished by study of Scripture (*Optatam Totius* §16). At the same time, critical academic study of Scripture was much more likely to receive the Vatican's imprimatur than in previous generations. Meanwhile in Europe (in the form of political theology) and in Latin America (in the form of liberation theology) the post–World War II period saw both Protestants and Catholics engaging

Scripture with fresh interest in a Christian social ethics that would place the problem of the poor front and center. Latin American liberation theology espoused a new hermeneutical principle, contending that the Bible speaks not only on behalf of the poor but also from their perspective; hence, the poor are in the best social location to understand Scripture. This idea, called "the epistemological privilege of the poor," was allied to the conviction that social location (and precommitments) shapes interpretation of the Bible. The appearance of liberation theology in the Western academy ushered in an era of perspectival interpretation. Various scholars began stressing that the influence of social location is not a problem to be overcome but rather is a necessary condition of interpretation that should be formalized as part of the hermeneutic process (see, e.g., Tolbert and Segovia). At the same time, the field of hermeneutics was overwhelmed by theoretical challenges. Whether in the dialogical forms espoused by Hans-Georg Gadamer and Paul Ricoeur or the deconstructionist brands associated with Jacques Derrida and Paul de Man, philosophical hermeneutics confronted Christian ethics with questions about the semantic clarity of texts and the location of meaning in texts, radicalizing the kinds of questions that earlier generations of Christians had tackled in discussing, for example, allegorical interpretation, the perspecuity of Scripture, and probabilism.

The interaction between liberationist and philosophical hermeneutics raised fresh questions about both the interpreter and the biblical text as factors in the hermeneutic process. If the church fathers and most theologians of the medieval and Reformation eras had assumed that in order to interpret rightly one needed to be well formed spiritually, and if the Enlightenment and its heirs had tended to emphasize the power of reason and the importance of "method" in interpretation, an increasing number of late-twentieth-century interpreters focused on the process by which the socially (or ideologically) conditioned interpreter constructs meaning out of a (somewhat or radically) "indeterminate" biblical text under the impulse of a certain interest (or precommitment). Recognizing that in a situation of multiple interpretive possibilities and competing human interests the interpreter must be regarded as a moral agent led to reflection on the "ethics of interpretation" (Elisabeth Schüssler Fiorenza, Daniel Patte).

Biblical scholarship also became increasingly sensitive to the role of literary or oral "form" in textual communication and the importance of considering the nature and purpose of a biblical text before using it as a basis for conclusions about ethics. Hence, one asked whether poetic descriptions of God's knowledge of the person in the womb (Ps. 139:13–16) were being used appropriately if made the basis for inferences about the moral status of the fetus or whether references to animal life in poetic descriptions designed to extol the greatness of the Creator (Ps. 104) warranted philosophical inferences about the moral status of living things in Christian versions of deep ecology. At the same time, many biblical interpreters were also developing a fresh appreciation for the way Scripture, in the variety of its genres (and not only or even primarily in ethical prescriptions), bears on ethics by shaping community Christian identity and providing insight into moral formation.

By the close of the twentieth century, the role of the Bible in Christian ethics had become a highly complex theological and intellectual problem. Except in fundamentalist circles, one could no longer simply equate biblical ethics with Christian ethics. The diversity of moral perspectives in Scripture and the epochal difference between antiquity and modernity (or postmodernity) made it difficult to conceive the Bible as a direct source of Christian ethics. This problem was only exacerbated by a growing perception that Scripture was not only a weapon against ideology (as Latin American liberation theology generally treated the Bible) but also a purveyor of it (as some feminist biblical interpreters contended). Hence, by the dawn of the twenty-first century, almost all participants in the discussion agreed that the Bible is in some sense an authority for Christian ethics, but conceptions of that authority—its force and scope—continued to vary widely.

Bibliography

Althaus, P. *The Ethics of Martin Luther*. Trans. Robert C. Schulz. Fortress, 1972.

Birch, B., and L. Rasmussen. *Bible and Ethics in the Christian Life*. Rev. ed. Augsburg, 1989.

Cosgrove, C. *Appealing to Scripture in Moral Debate: Five Hermeneutical Rules*. Eerdmans, 2002.

Curran, C. *American Catholic Social Ethics: Twentieth-Century Approaches*. University of Notre Dame Press, 1983.

de Groot, C., and M. Taylor, eds. *Recovering Nineteenth-Century Women Interpreters of the Bible*. SBLSymS 38. Society of Biblical Literature, 2007.

Estep, W. *The Anabaptist Story: An Introduction to Sixteenth-Century Anabaptism*. 3rd ed. Eerdmans, 1996.

Ferguson, E., ed. *Christian Life: Ethics, Morality, and Discipline in the Early Church*. SEC 16. Garland, 1993.

Fleming, J. *Defending Probabilism: The Moral Theology of Juan Caramuel*. Georgetown University Press, 2006.

Gorman, M. *Abortion and the Early Church: Christian, Jewish, and Pagan Attitudes in the Greco-Roman World*. InterVarsity, 1982.

Harakas, S. *Patristic Ethics*. Vol. 1 of *Wholeness of Faith and Life: Orthodox Christian Ethics*. Holy Cross Orthodox Press, 1999.

Harnus, J.-M. *It Is Not Lawful for Me to Fight: Early Christian Attitudes toward War, Violence, and the State*. Herald Press, 1980.

Hauser, A., and D. Watson, eds. *The Ancient Period*. Vol. 1 of *A History of Biblical Interpretation*. Eerdmans, 2003.

Helmholz, R. "The Bible in the Service of Canon Law." *Chicago-Kent Law Review* 70 (1995): 1557–81.

Jones, D. *Reforming the Morality of Usury: A Study of Differences That Separated the Protestant Reformers*. University Press of America, 2004.

Kuczynski, M. *Prophetic Song: The Psalms as Moral Discourse in Late Medieval England*. University of Pennsylvania Press, 1995.

Luthardt, C. *Geschichte der christlichen Ethik*. 2 vols. Dörffling & Franke, 1888–93.

Matter, E. *The Voice of My Beloved: The Song of Songs in Western Medieval Christianity*. University of Pennsylvania Press, 1990.

Ogletree, T. *The Use of the Bible in Christian Ethics: A Constructive Essay*. Fortress, 1983.

Shaw, T. *The Burden of the Flesh: Fasting and Sexuality in Early Christianity*. Fortress, 1998.

Siker, J. *Scripture and Ethics: Twentieth-Century Portraits*. Oxford University Press, 1997.

Swartley, W. *Slavery, Sabbath, War, and Women: Case Issues in Biblical Interpretation*. Herald Press, 1983.

Tolbert, M., and F. Segovia, eds. *Reading from This Place*. 2 vols. Fortress, 1995.

Walsh, K., and D. Wood, eds. *The Bible in the Medieval World: Essays in Memory of Beryl Smalley*. Basil Blackwell, 1985.

White, R. E. O. *Christian Ethics: The Historical Development*. John Knox, 1981.

♦ New Testament Ethics ♦

Charles H. Cosgrove

New Testament Ethics as a Discipline

Since the formation of a Christian Bible in the third and fourth centuries, preachers and teachers of the church have appealed to the Bible's authority in moral instruction and as a basis for Christian ethics. Only in the past 150 years or so has "New Testament ethics" been a subject distinct from theology or separate from the task of giving practical instruction to the church. Prior to the nineteenth century, attention to biblical teaching on moral subjects was found in works of theology, in separate treatises on ethics, and in a wide variety of other churchly writings devoted to instructing the faithful, but separate works on the subject of NT ethics scarcely existed. Certainly this was the case if NT ethics denotes a historical treatment of earliest Christian morality in its original environment as reflected by the writings that came to make up the NT. In a book published in 1899 on NT ethics, Hermann Jacoby remarked that he knew of only one antecedent to his historical approach to the subject, Albrecht Thoma's *Geschichte der christlichen Sittenlehre in der Zeit des Neuen Testaments* (1879). Thoma himself was aware of no prior study of first-century Christian morality in which the author treated the subject using modern historical methods. Perhaps these authors were unaware of George Matheson's *Landmarks of New Testament Morality* (1888) and like works or did not regard them as sufficiently historical in the rigorous "scientific" sense.

Some who study NT ethics use the terms *ethics* and *morality* as rough equivalents; others distinguish the two by defining ethics as rational reflection on moral questions. Wayne Meeks finds it helpful to conceive "morality" as "a pervasive but, often, only partly conscious set of value-laden dispositions, inclinations, attitudes, and habits," and "ethics" as a "reflective, second-order activity, morality made conscious" (Meeks, *Origins*, 4). A number of scholars have stressed that the NT contains little that can be described as "ethics" in this more precise sense, although NT morality can be analyzed for its underlying logic. For example, by attending to the often unspoken or only briefly expressed rationales that inform moral exhortation in the NT, one can work out something of the implicit ethics of the NT.

Although the word *ethics* is a plural noun, it is often used as a singular concept. As a result, it is not immediately clear whether "New Testament ethics" is a plural or singular subject. Today, most scholars recognize that the NT does not express a single "ethic," and studies of NT ethics typically are careful to describe the diversity of moral teachings and assumptions in the NT writings. Some (but not all) studies also make it a point to synthesize this diversity into some sort of unity.

Interest in a synthesis almost invariably involves the assumption that the use of the NT for Christian ethics is compromised if its various writings present no more than a jumble of diverse and even contradictory views. It is generally agreed, however, that unity is not immediately evident and needs to be demonstrated (or even "constructed"), and that the NT cannot be treated as a "rule book" with immediate applicability to contemporary moral questions. Conscientious use of the NT requires due attention to the variety of views and perspectives in its writings and the historical and cultural distance between its times and later times. That distance calls for some sort of hermeneutical translation or mediation.

This way of conceiving NT ethics reflects the highly influential biblical theology program of Johann Philipp Gabler (1753–1826), which continues to shape the way Christian scholars think about their role as academics. Gabler's program consisted of three basic parts: (1) historically sensitive interpretation of the various books of the Bible, treating each in its own terms; (2) synthesis of the results of this historical descriptive work, with the aid of general concepts; and (3) theological construction for contemporary life, carried out primarily by theologians who make use of the syntheses provided them by biblical scholars. The staying power of Gabler's program is especially evident in Richard Hays's *Moral Vision of the New Testament*, in which he proposes and carries out four tasks: the descriptive, the synthetic, the hermeneutical, and the pragmatic. Hays assumes the normative concept of "New Testament," seeks to show that there is a unity (with diversity and variety) in the NT's "moral vision," and engages himself in the constructive task (hermeneutical and pragmatic) of developing normative proposals for the contemporary church.

Not all treatments of the subject attempt to synthesize the ethical views of the NT, much less to tackle the question of how to use the NT in contemporary moral debate. A common approach is to confine the task to describing the moral instruction and assumptions of individual writings or "authorships" (Mark, Luke-Acts, the Pauline corpus, the Johannine writings, etc.). This approach, exemplified by Frank Matera's *New Testament Ethics*, may be termed narrowly historical because it does not attend to questions inherent to the use of the "New Testament" as Scripture. This is not to say that those who take a more narrowly historical approach to NT ethics are uninterested in the practical use of the NT, much less that they do not regard these writings as Scripture. Nevertheless, the narrowly historical approach reflects a certain ambiguity about whether the subject of NT ethics is the NT writings interpreted on their own terms and in their original historical settings before there was a NT, or whether "New Testament ethics" is an inherently theological and confessional concept that cannot be treated without certain assumptions about the nature of Scripture. The observation of this ambiguity becomes important when we consider that the moral teachings of the NT writings are also studied historically by those interested in giving an account of early Christian morality in general. Wayne Meeks uses the NT writings in this way in *The Origins of Christian Morality* and *The Moral World of the First Christians*. If one were to abstract from these books only what Meeks says about the NT writings, would that abstraction amount to "New Testament ethics"? Or is "New Testament ethics" something different, a subcategory of a theological discipline, analogous to the way in which Gabler conceived biblical theology as a subcategory of a broader theological task?

Another ambiguity touching the concept of NT ethics is whether it properly includes the ethics of the historical Jesus as distinct from the ethics of Jesus in the Gospels. Modern critical study of the NT distinguishes the historical Jesus from later portraits of him. Should descriptions of NT ethics include reconstructions of the ethics of the historical Jesus? In fact, the ethics of Jesus is included as a separate subject in books on NT ethics by Allen Verhey, Wolfgang Schrage, Rudolf Schnackenburg, and Russell Pregeant. But others (e.g., Hays, Matera) restrict themselves to the NT writings without offering separate reconstructions of Jesus' ethics. Hays explains that his book is not about the historical development of early Christian ethics but rather concerns the question of how the NT witnesses should shape the life of the church (Hays 158–59).

Hays's position is not the only one available to those who approach NT ethics as a theological discipline in service of Christian ethics. One can make a theological case that the historical Jesus is the proper presupposition of NT ethics and hence that the study of NT ethics should begin with the historical Jesus. This way of putting the matter recalls a famous mid-twentieth-century debate between Rudolf Bultmann and his student Ernst Käsemann. Bultmann argued that the historical Jesus is the presupposition of NT theology but not himself (his activity and teachings as reconstructed by scholarship) part of that theology (or of Christian theology generally). Käsemann insisted that the church has a legitimate interest in discovering the historical relation between the Jesus of history and the Jesus of the NT (the "Jesus of faith"), even if it would be wrong to make a reconstructed historical Jesus not only primary but also superior in authority to the Jesus of the NT. Certainly, there is no contradiction in the idea that both Jesus himself and the writings of the NT are authoritative for the church and should be taken together as foundations for Christian ethics, however their relationship is conceived and however difficult it may be to reconstruct the historical Jesus.

Those who are explicit about their theological assumptions and commitments sometimes explain why they begin with Jesus (e.g., Verhey), but some books on NT ethics that make the historical Jesus their first topic proceed as if no explanation were needed. The reason, no doubt, is that the history of NT scholarship, with its momentous turn to rigorous historical methods in the nineteenth century, led to a conception of the field of NT study as including three subjects: the historical Jesus and his mission, the formation of the early church (including the oral tradition), and the NT writings. Hence, Rudolf Schnackenburg's *Moral Teaching of the New Testament* (1962) begins with Jesus, moves to the early church, and then examines the individual NT authors.

Method in New Testament Moral Reasoning

Orientation to Example

In deliberative rhetoric, where the aim is to persuade the audience to adopt a certain course of action, proof from example (Gk. *paradeigma*, Lat. *exemplum*) is a typical form of argument. Paul's Letters often move into a deliberative mode; hence, it is not surprising that his exhortation sometimes includes examples and calls for "imitation" (*mimēsis*). Paul gives brief narrative summaries of Christ's exemplary action and presses believers to behave in similar ways (Rom. 15:3; 2 Cor. 8:9; Phil. 2:6–11). He also urges his churches to imitate him (1 Cor. 4:16–17; 10:31–11:1; Gal. 4:12; Phil. 3:17; 4:9; 1 Thess. 1:5–6) and regards others as worthy of imitation as well (2 Cor. 8:1–6; 1 Thess. 2:14; cf. 1 Tim. 4:12). The unity of word and example is evident in his admonition "Keep on doing the things that you have learned and received and heard and seen in me" (Phil. 4:9). Or as he puts it in 1 Cor. 4:17, Timothy will "remind you of my ways in Christ Jesus, as I teach them everywhere in every church." The Greek term for "ways" (*hodoi*) in this passage reflects the Hebrew sense of *halakah*, a word that means "walking" and was used to express teaching about right living. This idea is also found in 2 Pet. 2:21 ("way of righteousness"). In other places Paul uses a Greek word for "walking" (*peripateō*) to convey an ethical meaning: "walking in love" (Rom. 14:15); "walk in newness of life" (Rom. 6:4; see also Rom. 13:13; 2 Cor. 12:18; 1 Thess. 2:12). In the same vein, Acts refers to the gospel as "the Way," which shows how closely the message was associated with a way of living (Acts 9:2; 19:9, 23; 22:4; cf. Matt. 21:32; Mark 12:14). These terms for "walking" and "way" can be used of right ways of living and thinking (as in nearly all the preceding examples) or wrong ways (as in Acts 14:16; 1 Cor. 3:3; Phil. 3:18; Jas. 5:20).

Early Christians would have assumed that one purpose of the Gospels, as history or biography, was to display Jesus as a model to be imitated. This ancient way of understanding the Gospels is evident in Justin Martyr's description of early Christian worship. After lengthy reading of the "memoirs of the apostles" (Gospels) or the prophets, Justin says, the president of the church gets up and urges the people to imitate the good things that they have heard (*1 Apol.* 66.3–4). The unity of a teacher's word and example was axiomatic for ancient Mediterraneans (see, e.g., Quintilian, *Inst.* 2.2.8). Readers—hearers—of the Gospels would have taken for granted that Jesus teaches them through his word and his example. The unity of these two is especially evident in the Gospel of Matthew, where key terms help the reader see the correlations between Jesus' teachings and his actions (cf., e.g., 5:5 with 11:29; 5:7 with 9:27; 5:39 with 26:52). Regarded in this light, the closing command to make disciples of all peoples, "teaching them to obey everything that I have commanded you" (28:20), means to instruct others in Jesus' commandments as preserved in his teachings and exemplified in the stories about what he did and how he lived.

Orientation to the Particular

In the Greco-Roman philosophical tradition, moral analysis focuses on the nature of things and particularly "the good" inherent to the nature of the human being. That "good" is rationally determined, with the help of experience and observation. The good in this general and abstract sense is not the focal point of moral understanding for the NT writers. In only one place is the question of "the good" posed in anything like a general way: in the Matthean version of the story of the rich young man, Jesus responds, "Why do you ask me about what is good?" Jesus goes on to give not an abstract definition of the good but rather an admonition that the man should keep the commandments, sell his possessions, and follow Jesus (Matt. 19:16–22). Is this admonition meant for everyone or only for this man or those like him? However we answer this question, it is evident that Jesus' response speaks in the concrete and particular.

It is the nature of the example to be concrete and particular, but often the example cannot be imitated unless one first grasps its principle(s). This suggests that the implicit principles of moral examples in the NT should be regarded as primary material for constructing NT ethics. We are encouraged in this direction by the fact that examples often are given to illustrate or explain concepts. The parable of the merciful Samaritan is offered to define the concept of "love" as an obligation to the "neighbor" (Luke 10:25–37). The "grace" (kindness, generosity) of "our Lord Jesus" is explained through a description of how he became "poor" in order to make others "rich" (2 Cor. 8:9). In Heb. 11, "faith" (as a moral-spiritual disposition) is defined with a series of examples from Scripture. In Phil. 2 Paul offers the example of Jesus to sum up a set of qualities that the Philippians are to embody with one another: love, humility, unity, other-centeredness. Modern scholars have characterized Jesus' exemplary behavior in the Gospels (notably in his miracle-working and table fellowship) as "boundary-crossing" and animated by a special concern for the "marginalized." These concepts represent modern conceptual distillations of what are seen as implicit principles governing Jesus' mission.

Modes of Moral Reasoning

The NT writings contain moral exhortation but rarely take up ethical issues in reflective ways or offer comments about method in moral reasoning. Stoic philosophers, for example, were interested in debating the precise role to be given to precepts in moral thinking and exhortation (see, e.g., Seneca, *Ep.* 94). Nothing like this is found in the NT. The most sustained moral instruction appears in the Sermon on the Mount, but without articulation of informing assumptions. Only in Paul do we meet moral arguments where rationales are given, in his treatment of various topics in 1 Corinthians and in his counsel in Rom. 14–15 about issues between the "weak" and the "strong."

Using modern categories, we can ask whether the reasoning in and behind the NT conceptions of moral decision-making is primarily consequentialist (judgments in concrete cases based on best outcomes as evaluated by normative principles), deontological (judgments governed by moral rules without regard for consequences), virtue-based (judgments governed by good character), or some combination of these. But we get an idea of the methods of NT writers only by observing what they do. One finds teaching that seems to reflect a consequentialist approach in 1 Cor. 7:1–16 (advice about whether to marry or separate based on outcomes) and instruction that appears to assume a deontological approach in Mark 10:2–9 (a rule about divorce). Exhortations to imitate exemplars arguably belong to a virtue-based approach, especially since the NT writers take for granted that exemplars are found not only in Scripture but also in life as formative influences in community. It probably is fair to say that all the NT writers took for granted that moral formation depends on imitating good examples in Scripture and in life. It is also clear that disagreements about proper behavior were debated with recourse to a variety of modes of argument: appeal to authority (personal authority, rules, the Mosaic law, common opinion), appeal to character, and appeal to principles (including consequences judged by principles).

The NT writers expected the near end of the world, and most if not all believed that the new age (new creation, kingdom of God) had already begun in provisional ways. Animated by this eschatological consciousness, some early church leaders sought to live out in the present the ideals that they ascribed to the dawning future age. Paul was one such leader, although he also sought to restrain the tendencies of those (such as certain members of the churches at Corinth) who wished to live as if the new creation had already fully arrived. His declaration that in Christ the distinctions between Jew and Greek, male and female, slave and free come to an end (Gal. 3:28) seems to have influenced his understanding of the social order that ought to prevail in the church, making him something of an egalitarian. But he was a consistent champion of full equality in the present when it came to only one of these social relations. the equality of gentile with Jew. Moreover, in the NT generally, eschatological references in moral exhortation are almost always threats of future punishment or promises of reward; only occasionally do they entail explicit appeals to new norms based on a vision of the future kingdom or new creation.

Integrated Conceptions of the New Testament's Moral Vision

Modern interpreters interested in offering integrated descriptions of NT ethics have tended to focus on combining two main voices: Jesus and Paul. "Jesus" means the historical Jesus, the Jesus of the Synoptic Gospels, the Jesus of all four Gospels, or a portrait drawn on historical-Jesus research and the Gospels. "Paul" is usually restricted to the undisputed letters. Other parts of the NT are incorporated into the synthesis with various degrees of emphasis and attention to how well they fit into an ethical vision compounded of Jesus and Paul.

Integrating Jesus and Paul usually entails correlating Jesus' message of the kingdom ("reign") of God with Paul's understanding that a "new creation" has dawned in Christ. The Gospels frame Jesus' teaching by ordering it within the story of his journey to death and resurrection. Paul's Jesus, who willingly gave up his life out of obedience to God and merciful concern for others, seems to jibe with the other-centered Jesus of the Gospels, who embodies in action the values of the kingdom and who dies for what he said and how he lived. "Love" is the primary ethical principle for the Jesus of the Gospels and the Jesus of Paul, a love that Paul and the Gospels define as self-sacrificial and directed toward all human beings. Debate continues regarding the sense in which love is a primary moral norm in the NT and how far each writing or author is committed to an ethic based on love.

Bibliography

Burridge, R. *Imitating Jesus: An Inclusive Approach to New Testament Ethics*. Eerdmans, 2007.

Hays, R. *The Moral Vision of the New Testament: Community, Cross, New Creation; A Contemporary Introduction to New Testament Ethics*. HarperSanFrancisco, 1996.

Keck, L. "Rethinking 'New Testament Ethics.'" *JBL* 115 (1996): 3–16.

Matera, F. *New Testament Ethics*. Westminster John Knox, 1996.

Meeks, W. *The Moral World of the First Christians*. Westminster, 1986.

————. *The Origins of Christian Morality: The First Two Centuries.* Yale University Press, 1993.

Pregeant, R. *Knowing Truth, Doing Good: Engaging New Testament Ethics.* Fortress, 2008.

Schnackenburg, R. *The Moral Teaching of the New Testament.* Trans. J. Holland-Smith and W. O'Hara. Herder, 1965 [1962].

Schrage, W. *The Ethics of the New Testament.* Trans. D. Green. Fortress, 1988 [1982].

Verhey, A. *The Great Reversal: Ethics and the New Testament.* Eerdmans, 1984.

2

||||||||||||||||||||||||||||||||||||||||||||||||||||||||||||||||||||||||||||||||||||||||||

GOSPELS AND ACTS

♦ Matthew ♦

Robert L. Brawley

The author of the Gospel of Matthew is anonymous. The author does not appear in the text but in a later title. Scholars generally consider this Gospel a third-generation witness to Jesus that includes among its sources the Gospel of Mark and a sayings source known as Q. This view has led some to attempt to isolate material from the historical Jesus or from developments between Jesus and Matthew as sources for ethics. For example, some have concluded that Jesus opposed divorce, but Matthew contains a development whereby divorce is forbidden "except for adultery." Recognizing the narrative nature of Matthew, however, other scholars have shifted their emphasis to the Gospel's final form as a source for ethics. Still there are multiple approaches to how Matthew serves the enterprise of ethics. This essay deals particularly with extracting principles, imitating role models, the hermeneutics of suspicion, character formation, and deriving ethics from a relationship with God.

One approach is grounded in the commandments to love God and neighbor, because "on these two commandments hang all the law and the prophets" (22:40). As central as the two commandments are, they point to Scripture as a whole ("all the law and the prophets"). Thus, they are part of a grand plot

41

reaching back to Abraham in which God makes promises, such as blessing all the people of the earth, and acts to keep these promises alive.

Conventionally, the double "love commandment" is supplemented with Jesus' teachings, especially the Sermon on the Mount, parables, and direct commands. A long tradition takes the Beatitudes (5:3–12) as exhortations, although no imperatives occur until 5:12: "Rejoice and be glad" (in the midst of opposition). The outcome is a love ethic, an intensification of the law (e.g., broadening the interpretation of murder), and specific instructions on things such as divorce, with the assumption that Jesus' sayings interpret God's unchanging will.

Another approach takes characters as role models. This is reflected in the popular platitude "What would Jesus do?" On the one hand, Jesus demonstrates living under God's rule. The same is true of other characters, such as the Canaanite woman (15:22–28). But ordinarily the characters are too flawed to be role models. After Peter confesses Jesus as the Messiah and Son of God, for example, he plays a satanic role (16:13–23). But this case also shows that the norms of the narrative enable readers to distinguish Peter's appropriate from his inappropriate praxis. On the other hand, to make Jesus a role model presents readers with unattainable challenges (teacher, healer, divine agent). Further, Matthew's Jesus repeatedly surprises. What would Jesus do? Matthew's readers should probably confess, "We cannot say, because he would surprise us."

A hermeneutics of suspicion asks if Matthew's rhetoric may be a part of sustaining injustices. Does Matthew give a derogatory portrayal of the Jews (e.g., 27:25)? Are women portrayed passively, and is their prominence among the followers of Jesus suppressed (e.g., 10:2–4)?

Such approaches tend to isolate commandments, God's will, role models, and suspicious perspectives from the framework of God's reign. Matthew establishes this framework early. It appears in the proclamation of John the Baptist (3:2). Then 4:17 is programmatic: "From that time Jesus began to proclaim, 'Repent, for the kingdom of heaven has come near.'" Henceforth, Jesus proclaims God's kingdom. When he begins the Sermon on the Mount nine verses later, he is interpreting God's kingdom. If the Beatitudes are taken as exhortations, they no longer reflect instances of God's rule, and rather than the outcome of God's rule, they become conditions for entering God's kingdom.

The communal nature of these relationships is an important part of several approaches to ethics in Matthew, including character ethics. Character ethics holds that the community's use of Scripture shapes the character of people who are nurtured in its life. Someone steeped in Matthew's story will likely have an orientation toward life quite distinct from the prevailing culture.

Another option is that Matthew mediates encounters with God out of which the community lives. For these relationships Matthew uses particularly kinship language: a "Father" in relationship with children who are brothers and sisters. Agricultural metaphors also reflect these relationships ("trees bearing fruit"). Beginning with these relationships means that ethics in Matthew is not merely determining appropriate praxis but is preeminently a matter of the source, motivation, and empowerment for living. When God is the source, motivation, and empowerment, living appropriately is the fruit of God's rule. For example, when God is parent, God's children love their enemies (5:45).

In several cases Matthew speaks of "righteousness" (*dikaiosyne*). On the one hand, this means a right relationship with God, and its other side is ethics. But English poses difficulties in representing *dikaiosyne*, because it also means "justice." So seeking *dikaiosyne* also means seeking justice. Additionally, seeking justice alone may be inadequate. Joseph, on the basis of justice (1:19), wishes to put Mary away quietly. His motivation is not deficient, but his understanding of God's purposes is, and so he intends to act at cross-purposes with God. Consequently, God informs Joseph what the divine purposes are. Thus, God's rule is not only the motivation or empowerment for praxis but also a source beyond what may be written. Because ethical praxis depends on God, ethics remains open to God's future.

Finally, justice has a particularly acute meaning in the context of the Roman Empire, which claimed to have established justice in the world. Imperial rule operated through collaboration of client kings and local elites, such as Herodian rulers and the Judean council. For Matthew, the rule of God is an alternative to this system that Rome called justice.

Bibliography

Burridge, R. *Imitating Jesus: An Inclusive Approach to New Testament Ethics.* Eerdmans, 2007.

Carter, W. *Matthew and the Margins: A Sociopolitical and Religious Reading.* Orbis, 2000.

Fowl, S., and L. Jones. *Reading in Communion: Scripture and Ethics in Christian Life.* Eerdmans, 1991.

Hays, R. *The Moral Vision of the New Testament: Community, Cross, and New Creation; A Contemporary Introduction to New Testament Ethics.* HarperSanFrancisco, 1996.

Wink, W. *Engaging the Powers: Discernment and Resistance in a World of Domination.* Fortress, 1992.

Mark

Robert L. Brawley

The author of the Gospel of Mark is anonymous, although early tradition held that Mark wrote Peter's memoirs. The name *Mark* appears in a later title rather than the text. This is the earliest Gospel, and its sources are unknown. Interpreters have used methods such as the following for deriving ethics from Mark.

Extracting norms for judging people and events. In Sabbath controversies, human welfare takes precedence over Sabbath restrictions; stated positively, it is lawful to do good on the Sabbath (3:4). Sabbath legality no longer proscribes activity but prescribes redemptive activity. The commandment is still valid, but it alone is not decisive. Similarly, the rich man's use of possessions in 10:17–23 qualifies keeping commandments.

Determining bases for evaluating motivation, purposes, and objectives. As an act of faith, a bleeding woman violates social norms and touches Jesus to be made well (5:25–34). Out of compassion, Jesus feeds the hungry (6:34–44; 8:1–9). Jesus teaches forgiveness as a basis for relationships with others and with God (11:25).

Cultivating virtues. In the Aristotelian tradition, some interpreters look for virtues to practice to build character. Does perseverance in suffering strengthen faith and facilitate moral development (e.g., 4:19)? Is sacrifice to the point of death vicarious for others (8:34–35)?

Discovering Jesus' ethical teachings. After a discussion with some stereotyped Pharisees, Jesus teaches that a man who sends his wife away and marries another commits adultery (10:11). But more than teach about life, Jesus restores life (3:1–5). Further, rather than repeat Jesus' teachings, recipients and witnesses of Jesus' healings bear testimony to Jesus' activity as God's doing.

Finding critiques of people, systems, and structures that perpetuate injustice, and envisioning justice. Jesus' programmatic proclamation of the advent of God's kingdom (1:15) means, on the one hand, a critique of other kingdoms. On the other hand, if God rules, then ethical correlates are predicated of humans who live under God's rule. Restorations of the "unclean" to normal society (like the Gerasene demoniac [5:2–15]) implicitly critique social marginalization. Conversely, restorations of marginalized people to the social order dramatize God's rule. Mark evaluates negatively the execution of John the Baptist under Herod Antipas and Herodias, who are collaborators with the Roman Empire, and who see their elite status as exempting them from social propriety and as empowering them to execute John over a grudge (6:17–29). Following Jesus is an alternative to rulers of imperial systems

(10:42–45). The high priestly party consists of ruling elites (who inevitably collaborate with the empire) against whom Jesus makes a claim on the temple (11:15–18; 12:1–12). Similarly, Jesus critiques scribal abuse of legal systems (12:38–40) and anticipates that following him will cause retribution from imperial collaborators—councils, synagogues, governors, and kings (13:9–20). This materializes immediately in his crucifixion implicating the governor, scribal systems, and the high priestly party (14:1–15:31).

Locating ethics in God's will for humanity and the world. The parable of the sower in 4:3–20 presents living under God's rule as analogous to seed in good earth that stands over against seed in unproductive soil—that is, over against evil. Similarly, living under God's rule is like the earth producing a harvest from growing seed (4:28–29).

Living in response to God. Mark points beyond its own story for living. First, Mark elicits a relationship with God that transcends its own narrative. When Jesus and a scribe agree that the greatest commandment is to love God and neighbor (12:28–34), Mark evokes a relationship with God that is inseparable from a relationship with other people. Mark also anticipates readers who will encounter God in reading the narrative. Living in response to God is not arbitrary, as it is subject to communal confirmation and has to do with the God characterized in Mark and the biblical tradition on which it draws. Because relationships with God are the source, motivation, and empowerment for praxis, ethics means giving up knowing in advance what one is to do. Praxis deriving from God also goes beyond Mark's story because it is impossible to know what love looks like until one confronts concrete situations. An instance is Jesus' "Abba" prayer that he may derive his behavior from the God to whom he is related as a son to a father (14:35–36). Some interpreters take this prayer as an example for imitation, but if so, it is noticeably ineffective for the disciples who fall asleep while Jesus is at prayer.

The Gospel of Mark points beyond itself because it anticipates following Jesus into the future beyond the end of the story. On the one hand, Mark is full of failure. The disciples regularly miss the mark; a widow casts all her livelihood into the temple treasury (12:41–44), but the very next verses inform readers about the temple's destruction (13:1–2); a woman anoints Jesus royally but for his burial (14:3–9); when Jesus is arrested, his gathering of followers disintegrates when they run away (14:27, 50). On the other hand, over against this failure and collapse, God remains Lord in a world that can turn into chaos. Further, Mark points to disciples following the risen Jesus beyond the end of the story (16:7).

Interpreters tend to characterize God by values. For instance, God is a God of justice. True enough, but the God of Mark's Gospel is primarily a God who acts and whose power gives life. This power of God at work beyond the end of Mark is the good earth out of which the seed bears fruit.

Bibliography

Burridge, R. *Imitating Jesus: An Inclusive Approach to New Testament Ethics*. Eerdmans, 2007.

Fowl, S., and L. Jones. *Reading in Communion: Scripture and Ethics in Christian Life*. Eerdmans, 1991.

Hays, R. *The Moral Vision of the New Testament: Community, Cross, and New Creation; A Contemporary Introduction to New Testament Ethics*. HarperSanFrancisco, 1996.

Matera, F. *New Testament Ethics: The Legacies of Jesus and Paul*. Westminster John Knox, 1996.

Via, D. *The Ethics of Mark's Gospel—in the Middle of Time*. Fortress, 1985.

♦ Luke ♦

Robert L. Brawley

Luke's Gospel is anonymous, although the tradition has associated this writing with Luke, Paul's sometime companion (mentioned in, e.g., Phlm. 24). Assuming that Luke was the author of this Gospel and further that this Luke was in fact Paul's companion offers little to the interpreter. More productive is careful engagement with the text of Luke, together with comparison with Luke's sources (usually regarded as including Mark's Gospel and a sayings source known as Q) and Acts (Luke's second volume). For example, as a unit, Luke-Acts emphasizes the use of possessions as demonstrative of one's relationship with God.

Luke 4:18–19 maps Jesus' program in words borrowed from Isa. 58:6; 61:1–2: good news for the poor, release to captives, sight for the blind, freedom for the oppressed. Another programmatic Lukan text defines Jesus' ministry as the good news of God's kingdom (4:43). From the kingdom's centrality, it follows that "blessed are you poor" is thematic: "yours is the kingdom of God" (6:20). When God rules, the marginalized move from disdain in the social order to blessedness.

Often overlooked is that the Roman Empire as context permeates Luke. Luke 3:1–2 portrays the way the empire trickles down from the emperor through governors, client kings, and elite collaborators. Luke 22:25–26 explicitly presents

God's kingdom as an alternative to the empire. Jesus says to his disciples, "The kings of the nations lord it over them; and those in authority over them are called benefactors. But not so with you." The woes to the rich, satisfied, and prominent (6:24–26) fit an imperial context where they correspond to elite collaborators. The first woe (6:24) is not a reversal but an astounding devaluation of status and possessions: "You have received your consolation." But does the God who inverts the woes of the poor and for whom nothing is impossible (1:37) invert the woes of the rich? God is kind to the ungrateful and the wicked (6:35)—the types to whom Jesus addresses the woes.

Division into winners and losers is a false dichotomy in Luke, as people under judgment have the possibility of entering God's kingdom. Does Jesus cultivate opponents like gardeners cultivate fig trees so that they might bear fruit (13:6–9)? In the parable of the prodigal son (15:11–32), the father with his older son is like a gardener cultivating a fig tree. Does the older son change and rejoice over the return of his disgraced brother? Is Jesus persuasive? At least some scribes agree with him in 20:39.

Some interpreters charge Luke with anti-Semitism. But early on, John the Baptist contrasts the offspring of vipers with true children of Abraham; furthermore, the God for whom nothing is impossible can make stones (even offspring of vipers) into Abraham's children (3:7–8). Repeatedly, controversy stories are open-ended and anticipate that opponents may become God's children. Moreover, marginalized people are continually reintegrated into Judean society.

One approach to Scripture and ethics identifies five ways biblical materials inform ethics: (1) moral law, (2) principles, (3) analogies to contemporary situations, (4) understanding of the world and human beings, and (5) understanding of God. But in Luke these all point more to the source, motivation, and empowerment for ethics than to explicit directives for praxis.

(1) Luke is weak in appeals to moral law for ethics. The law informs piety more than ethics (1:6; 2:22, 27).

(2) The lawyer in 10:25–37 epitomizes the law as love of God and neighbor embedded in each other. But his question "Who is my neighbor?" quibbles with definitions, anticipates no action, and shows that principles as such do not translate into ethics.

(3) Analogies with Jesus' followers enable readers to discover characters with whom they identify primarily in their deficiencies and in whom they can witness the realization of God's rule, but hardly people they should emulate. If one looks for characters to emulate, then Mary's positive response in her trouble, perplexity, and fear (1:29–30, 38) qualifies her as one of the best. But in the immediate story of Jesus' birth and also in the larger story of the restoration

of God's people, the issue is how *God* is at work in human trouble, perplexity, and fear. When the disciples oppose bringing infants to Jesus, readers can hardly imitate them; nevertheless, they are part of a concrete demonstration of how God's rule is being realized (18:15–17).

(4) The understanding of the world and human beings and (5) the understanding of God invade each other. The narrator's perspective is that who humans are and what they do depend on who the God with whom they are in relationship is and what this God does. This emphasis anticipates ethics—not directives but a relationship with God as mediated through Luke that is the fountain for praxis. This is not to neglect action by hiding behind something that precedes ethics; rather, relationship with God bears fruit, often in ways that God's children cannot anticipate. In the parable of the so-called good Samaritan, love of God means love of neighbor (10:25–37). Loving God bears fruit in the Samaritan's actions that are dangerous (brigands are threatening) and that unexpectedly cross social, ethnic, and religious boundaries. Reality is transformed because the understanding of the world and a relationship with God invade each other. Not only does praxis determine relationships; relationships underlie praxis.

Bibliography

Burridge, R. *Imitating Jesus: An Inclusive Approach to New Testament Ethics*. Eerdmans, 2007.

Carter, W. *The Roman Empire and the New Testament: An Essential Guide*. Abingdon, 2006.

Fowl, S., and L. Jones. *Reading in Communion: Scripture and Ethics in Christian Life*. Eerdmans, 1991.

Hays, R. *The Moral Vision of the New Testament: Community, Cross, and New Creation; A Contemporary Introduction to New Testament Ethics*. HarperSanFrancisco, 1996.

Matera, F. *New Testament Ethics: The Legacies of Jesus and Paul*. Westminster John Knox, 1996.

⬧ John ⬧

Robert L. Brawley

The identity of the author of the Fourth Gospel remains obscure. An author appears in the text as the "disciple" (21:24), but little can be verified about this witness. The dominant view among NT scholars is that John is the product of communal development of tradition, whoever its final redactor might have been.

Rather than seeing John's Gospel as a source for ethics, many have accused John of loving Christians and hating Jews. John is charged with characterizing Jews as children of the devil and as unbelievers (8:44–45). Granted, in the history of interpretation John has been shamefully used against Jewish people. But is such usage of John appropriate? Nowhere does John mention hating Jews. Hatred is expressed only the other way around: the world hates Jesus and his followers. Furthermore, when Jesus tells some Jews that they are from their father the devil, he does not characterize Judaism. Specific Jewish characters are not the Jewish people; rather, they are some Jews who are actually identified earlier as believers (8:31). This text is quite important for Johannine ethics because, for John, what one is and does derives from a relationship with a parent: either the devil or God. The text characterizes behavior, not Jews or "the Jewish people." Furthermore, against the notion that John is anti-Jewish, Jesus is called "king of the Jews" (19:19), and he dies for the nation in order to gather dispersed Israelites (11:51–52).

One approach to biblical ethics focuses on moral law. For John, law should not be broken (7:23). However, law alone is insufficient. It must be interpreted and practiced appropriately, and it is subject to misuse (19:7). Many interpreters take Jesus' reference to "your law" in 8:17; 10:34 as distancing Jesus from the Jewish law. More likely, just as Moses appeals to Israelites on the basis of the "Lord your God" (e.g., Deut. 4:10), Jesus appeals to his interlocutors on the basis of their fundamental obligation to their own law. But in such a case the law reveals deficiencies more than produces rectitude. Furthermore, grace and truth go beyond law (1:17). The fact that the story of the woman caught in adultery (7:51–8:11) does not appear in the earliest and best manuscripts has not kept it from being used as a basis for qualifying law with mercy (see 7:23).

For many interpreters, John is more attuned with grounding living in principles, particularly belief, truth, and love. In fact, love becomes a "new commandment" from Jesus (13:34). But in light of other metaphors (shepherd and sheep, vine and branches), belief, truth, and love hardly remain "principles"; rather, they point to believing, truth, and love as relationships.

Emulating characters is difficult in John in that the characters frequently are ambiguous (Nicodemus affirms Jesus' identity and signs but does not understand his teaching or receive his testimony [3:1–14]), faulty (a man whom Jesus heals gives him away [5:15]), unable to understand (Peter refuses to let Jesus wash his feet [13:8–10]), and disloyal (Peter denies Jesus [18:25–27]). According to many translations, however, in washing his disciples' feet Jesus gives an "example" (*hypodeigma* [13:15]) for how they should live. Although *hypodeigma* frequently means "example," here it evokes considerations surpassing an example to be imitated. The foot-washing is to be understood only in the future (Jesus' resurrection?). A lack of understanding is rarely problematic for imitation. Moreover, the anticipated outcome is mutuality, not one-way imitation. Against a Jewish background, *hypodeigma* may be rendered "revelatory pattern."

John provides bases for critiquing social norms. Jesus' interaction with a Samaritan woman contravenes norms of gender and ethnicity (John 4:1–42). Sabbath controversies likewise imply critiques of norms. Jesus rejects the marginalization of a man born blind as a social anomaly ("sin" [9:1–3]). John also undermines imperialism. At Jesus' trial Pilate asks a basic Johannine question: "Where are you from?" (19:9). Given the thematic development of Jesus' origin, his response subordinates imperial power to God.

John's portrayal of reality is heavily symbolic. Reality is viewed in terms of sharp oppositions: light/darkness, above/below, truth/falsehood, eternal life/death. On the negative side, visual, spatial, and temporal dimensions of reality imply complicity in evil: "And this is the judgment, that the light has come into the world, and people loved darkness rather than light because their deeds were evil" (3:19). Human behavior is influenced by relationships with such dimensions of reality.

The positive axis of these oppositions corresponds to a relationship with God in which God is the source, motivation, and empowerment for ethics: "But those who do what is true come to the light, so that it may be clearly seen that their deeds have been done in God" (3:21). When people ask, "What must we do to perform the works of God?" (6:28), Jesus presents himself as the middle term through which human beings live in a relationship with God.

One purpose of John is to engender an encounter with Jesus (20:31). Ethics as the fruit of a relationship with Jesus and with God is inseparable from this encounter. Repeatedly, this relationship is described as "following," but other metaphors reflect encounters with Jesus and living in a mutuality with him. The good shepherd knows his own, and his own know him (10:14). Jesus is the vine; his disciples are the branches (15:5). He abides in them and they in him, and this relationship bears fruit (15:4).

Bibliography

Carter, W. *John: Storyteller, Interpreter, Evangelist.* Hendrickson, 2006.

Hays, R. *The Moral Vision of the New Testament: Community, Cross, and New Creation; A Contemporary Introduction to New Testament Ethics.* HarperSan-Francisco, 1996.

Matera, F. *New Testament Ethics: The Legacies of Jesus and Paul.* Westminster John Knox, 1996.

Rensberger, D. *Johannine Faith and Liberating Community.* Westminster, 1988.

Schneiders, S. *Written That You May Believe: Encountering Jesus in the Fourth Gospel.* Crossroad, 2003.

Thompson, M. *The God of the Gospel of John.* Eerdmans, 2001.

◆ Acts ◆

Robert L. Brawley

The author of the Acts of the Apostles is unknown to us, but is likely the same person who wrote the Gospel of Luke. Although the tradition has identified the author as Luke, Paul's sometime companion (see, e.g., Phlm. 24), that proposal offers us little help in actually interpreting the narrative. Thus, the promise of the Spirit spans both volumes, but Paul in Acts is not coordinated with Paul's letters. God's kingdom is less prominent in Acts than in Luke; nonetheless, the risen Jesus, Philip, Barnabas, and Paul proclaim God's kingdom. Thus, believing communities are aspects of God's rule, so that in the following approaches ethics is not merely individual but communal.

(1) In Acts law identifies deficient behavior (2:23; 7:53; 13:39), enhances reputations (5:34), demonstrates piety (21:20, 24; 22:12), affects relationships between Judeans and gentiles (10:28), but does not prescribe praxis. One exception is the Jerusalem decree for gentiles to abstain from sexual immorality (15:29; 21:25).

(2) Acts advocates values that imply praxis. Magic (13:6–11; 19:19), divination (16:16), and idolatry (14:15; 17:16–31) are renounced; their counterpart is belief. Substantial importance falls on the use of possessions. Lying to God by defrauding the community in regard to possessions has drastic consequences (5:1–10). Trying to buy God's gifts is reprehensible (8:19–20). Holding everything in common and distributing according to need reflect how the community is related to God (2:44–45). Giving alms receives positive evaluations (10:4, 31; 24:17), although, for some interpreters, giving alms stands in tension with distributing according to need. The latter expresses parity, whereas benefactors and beggars perpetuate "paternalistic humanitarianism."

(3) Characters such as Peter, Paul, Lydia, Dorcas, Stephen, and Cornelius play such positive roles that many interpreters make them models of praxis. Some translations of 20:35 imply that Paul makes himself an "example." But Paul's statement is expressed using a Greek verb (no noun corresponds

to "example") more adequately rendered "teaching by indication": "that by such work we must support the weak." Models serve as analogies for readers, but analogies break down when pushed toward their limits (e.g., raising the dead). Further, the characters themselves reflect the origin of what they do in God (3:12, 16). Still, readers can identify with characters in their deficiencies (Peter's reluctance to go to Cornelius [10:20, 28]) and can envision models of God in relation to humanity. If analogies are used to envision roles of ministry, a quotation from Joel clarifies that the first preachers included both women and men (2:11, 17–18).

(4) Acts construes a world centered on God, who is manifest in unusual phenomena: resurrection appearances, the coming of the Spirit with aural and visual analogies, speaking in tongues, divine plans for events and history. Praxis is repeatedly determined by interpreting Scripture or special revelation from the Spirit. God is strongly characterized as a God of power (1:7–8; 2:11) who changes relationships among people. Prominent among these is the surpassing of ethnic limits: "In every nation anyone who fears [God] and does what is right is acceptable to him" (10:35).

(5) Because Acts depicts the emerging identity of a new group, it is especially suitable for demonstrating the convergence of philosophical, feminist, and sociological theories concerning identity as a source for ethics. All three disciplines emphasize the relational character of identity. Identity emerges in community, changes by social patterns, and is sustained in relationships of solidarity.

Pentecost is a case in point (chap. 2). Here it is possible to see how identity, as it is embedded in social identity, is a source for praxis. If a group number is small, a substantial factor of power is needed for social identity. The conferring of the Holy Spirit is described as the reception of such power (1:8). Moreover, when the Holy Spirit comes (2:1–4), then according to thematic development from Luke 11:13 through Luke 24:49, the group assumes identity as God's children who receive the promise of the Spirit from their divine parent. The essential component of the unfolding identity is their relationship with God.

An ethical consequence of this identity might, at first glance, be called "distributive justice." But distribution according to need differs from conventional distributive justice (2:44–45). Distributive justice presumes normal institutional structures. The early Jerusalem community establishes itself as an alternative to existing structures. No consideration is given to how important specific functions are for the common good, as alleged when executives are compensated out of proportion to employees. Conventionally, lower classes work for the benefit of higher classes; Acts reverses the exchange. People at higher levels sell their possessions for redistribution to people at lower levels. This is no longer distributive justice but "differential justice."

(6) Acts is often considered an accommodation to the Roman Empire. But new sensitivity to how empire is experienced raises awareness of how the believing community is an alternative to empire. Acts reflects how imperial power filters down through governors, client kings, and elite collaborators. Noticing the collaboration of the people and the intersection of government and religion in the case of Herod Agrippa I in 12:20–23 sharpens awareness of how virtually everyone (regrettably) collaborates with oppressive systems. Even opponents recognize that Paul and Silas, by proclaiming another king, Jesus, act against the emperor (17:7). When Paul's Roman citizenship protects him from being flogged, it demonstrates inequality in Rome's judicial system (22:24–25). When Paul speaks to Felix about justice and self-control (24:25), Felix's fear shows that Paul expounds not abstract virtues but criteria for imperial agents. Felix's desire for a bribe in 24:26 confirms the need. Finally, Paul's appeal to the emperor in 25:11 is not an expression of confidence in the notorious Nero, but is a way out of the collaboration between ruling Judean elites and Festus (25:9–12).

Bibliography

Fowl, S., and L. Jones. *Reading in Communion: Scripture and Ethics in Christian Life*. Eerdmans, 1991.

Hays, R. *The Moral Vision of the New Testament: Community, Cross, and New Creation; A Contemporary Introduction to New Testament Ethics*. HarperSanFrancisco, 1996.

Johnson, L. *The Literary Function of Possessions in Luke-Acts*. SBLDS 39. Scholars Press, 1977.

Matera, F. *New Testament Ethics: The Legacies of Jesus and Paul*. Westminster John Knox, 1996.

Phillips, T., ed. *Acts and Ethics*. NTM 9. Sheffield Phoenix Press, 2005.

3

PAULINE EPISTLES

♦ Romans ♦

Victor Paul Furnish

This letter, addressed to a church that Paul had not founded, was dispatched from Corinth shortly before the apostle headed east with an offering from his gentile congregations for the Jewish Christians of Jerusalem (15:25–27, 30–31). His aims were to gain support for a projected mission to Spain (1:8–15; 15:23–24, 28–29, 32) and to address the problem of reported tensions between Jewish and gentile Christians in the imperial capital (14:1–15:6). These objectives account for Romans being the most deliberately and comprehensively theological of Paul's Letters. The apostle has laid out with special care the principal affirmations of his preaching and emphasized that the gospel is good news for gentiles as well as for Jews. As a result, the letter's argument also anticipated his impending trip to Jerusalem, where his gentile mission was being seriously questioned.

In the body of Romans Paul deals, in turn, with humanity's plight (1:18–3:20), contending that "all have sinned and fall short of the glory of God" (3:23), God's saving grace (3:21–8:39), God's faithfulness (chaps. 9–11), and God's claim (12:1–15:6). His premise, stated in 1:16–17, is that the gospel (God's power for salvation) reveals God's justice ("righteousness") "through

55

faith for faith," not only to Jews but also to gentiles. Concluding (15:7–13), he reiterates this universal scope of God's saving power, identifying Christ as "a servant of the circumcised on behalf of the truth of God in order that he might confirm the promises given to the patriarchs, and in order that the Gentiles might glorify God for his mercy" (15:8–9).

In accord with his belief in the universality of both humanity's sin and God's mercy, Paul identifies Christ's death for the "ungodly" and "sinners" as proof of God's unconditional love, an eschatological event of saving power (5:1–11). Baptism into Christ's death marks the crucifixion of one's "old self," deliverance from sin, and a transformed life under the dominion of grace (6:1–14). The first and most fundamental imperatives of the letter appear in this context, joined with a reference to the believers' new, eschatological existence: "No longer present your members to sin as instruments of wickedness, but present yourselves to God as those who have been brought from death to life, and present your members to God as instruments of righteousness" (6:13). Subsequently, Paul describes this new life as indwelt and guided by the Spirit (8:1–27).

The summons for believers to present themselves to God is reiterated in 12:1–2, where Paul introduces the ethical appeals that follow as grounded in the gospel that he has been expounding. Those who have been brought "from death to life" and granted a renewed mind are called to "discern" (*dokimazō*) what God regards as "good and acceptable and perfect." Paul's verb points to a process of inquiry, critical reflection, analysis, and testing that seeks to determine what God's will requires. It is clear from both the general appeals in chaps. 12–13 and the specific counsels in 14:1–15:6 that he regards the "norming norm" of moral discernment to be not God's law as conveyed in the Torah but rather God's love revealed in Christ (12:9–10; 14:15). Viewed through the lens of faith, all of the commandments of the law are perceived as summed up in the single commandment to love one's neighbor as oneself (13:8–10; cf. Gal. 5:13–14).

The appeals in 12:3–13, focused on conduct within the believing community, echo the apostle's comments in 1 Cor. 12–14 about membership in the body of Christ and its upbuilding in love. Most, if not all, of the counsels in 12:14–21 deal with the conduct of believers in relation to nonbelievers, including the church's opponents. Here again, love appears as the "norming norm": "Do not be overcome by evil, but overcome evil with good" (12:21).

One of the most difficult and debated passages in Romans is 13:1–7, which concerns the responsibility of Christians toward the governing authorities. Although some interpreters argue that Paul urges complete and unquestioning obedience to the state, there is better evidence for the view that he calls for compliance with its laws only in some limited sense. This passage may be seen as extending his appeal to live peaceably with all people (12:18); now he includes the governing authorities. He urges respect for these officials and the laws that they administer because he believes that God has authorized them for the specific purpose of rewarding those who do good and punishing those who do evil. He does not consider how believers should respond if the authorities prove unfaithful, unwise, or unjust in fulfilling this task. It is especially important that, like all of the counsels in these chapters, his call to good citizenship is fundamentally qualified by the introductory appeals: believers are to present their transformed lives unconditionally to God and not be conformed to this present age.

Only in 14:1–15:6 does Paul address an issue specific to the Roman church. The ("strong") gentile Christian majority despised the ("weak") Jewish Christian minority for abstaining from meat and observing special holy days, while the latter passed judgment on the former because they did not do so (cf. 1 Cor. 8:1–11:1). The apostle charges each group to "welcome" the other because both have been welcomed by God, and God alone will be their judge (14:2–4, 10–13). He believes, nonetheless, that the "strong" bear a special responsibility for the "weak": "If your brother or sister is being injured by what you eat, you are no longer walking in love. Do not let what you eat cause the ruin of one for whom Christ died" (14:15 [cf. 15:1–4]).

Bibliography

Betz, H. "The Foundations of Christian Ethics according to Romans 12:1–2." Pages 55–72 in *Witness and Existence: Essays in Honor of Schubert M. Ogden*, ed. P. Devenish and G. Goodwin. University of Chicago Press, 1989.

du Toit, A. "Shaping a Christian Lifestyle in the Roman Capital." Pages 167–97 in *Identity, Ethics, and Ethos in the New Testament*, ed. J. van der Watt. De Gruyter, 2006.

Keck, L. *Romans*. ANTC. Abingdon, 2005.

◆ 1 Corinthians ◆

David G. Horrell

First Corinthians was written by Paul, from Ephesus (1 Cor. 16:8), sometime between 49 and 55 CE. The authenticity of the letter is not seriously doubted, and most scholars accept its literary unity. It forms part of an ongoing communication between Paul and the Corinthian community. After his initial visit to Corinth, Paul has already written a letter (1 Cor. 5:9), and the Corinthians have written to Paul (1 Cor. 7:1). First Corinthians responds to this written communication and also to oral reports that have been brought to Paul (1 Cor. 1:11; 11:18). Further (more anguished) visits and letters follow 1 Corinthians (2 Cor. 2:1–4; 10–13) before an apparent reconciliation restores the relationship sufficiently for Paul's collection project (1 Cor. 16:1–4; Gal. 2:10) to be revitalized and completed (Rom. 15:25–27; 2 Cor. 8–9).

The character of 1 Corinthians as a response to issues raised in both letter and oral report makes it full of topics of ethical (and sociological) interest but also makes it a letter in which it is hard to discern an overall direction and focus of argument. More than any other Pauline letter, 1 Corinthians is full of Paul's responses to specific issues of conduct and conflict, full of ethics in a broad sense. The opening four chapters are dominated by the theme of divisions at Corinth. Chapters 5–7 deal with issues of sexual ethics and marriage, chapters 8–10 with the question of food offered to idols. Chapters 11–14 broadly deal with issues relating to the worship of the community: head coverings for women (11:2–16), the Lord's Supper (11:17–34), and the proper use of spiritual gifts (chaps. 12–14). Chapter 15 addresses the subject of the resurrection, while chapter 16 deals with various practical matters and greetings. It is notable that at least two of these major ethical sections (chaps. 8–10; 12–14) are structured in an A-B-A pattern in which the central section presents a paradigm for ethical action that fundamentally informs the response to the topic under discussion: Paul's example in renouncing his rights for the sake of others (9:1–23) is a model to the Corinthian "strong" (8:9–13); love (13:1–13) is a crucial foundation for the proper exercise of any spiritual gift.

Scholars have debated what are the main sources of influence on the ethics of 1 Corinthians. Some have argued that the Jewish Scriptures and interpretative traditions fundamentally shape the pattern of Paul's instruction. Others have pointed out parallels between Paul's treatment of ethical topics (such as sex and marriage) and the discussions of such issues in popular Greco-Roman moral philosophy, especially among Stoics and Cynics. There are significant differences of view on such matters, but it seems reasonably clear that Paul's moral thought is shaped both by the Jewish scriptural tradition and by the philosophical discussions of his day; it is the relative weight and specific influences that are harder to determine. But whatever the influence of such sources and ethical traditions, it is clear that Paul reconfigures such influences around the central key to his ethics: Christ. Even here there are various possible strands to disentangle. Some have argued that Jesus' teaching specifically permeates and informs Paul's ethical instruction. First Corinthians is indeed unusual among the Pauline letters in including three of the four most widely agreed references to

Jesus' teaching in Paul's writings: 7:10–11, referring to the teaching on divorce (Mark 10:2–12 // Matt. 19:3–9; Matt. 5:31–32 // Luke 16:18); 9:14, alluding to the mission charge instructions (Matt. 10.10 // Luke 10:7); and 11:23–24, citing the tradition of Jesus' words at the Last Supper (Mark 14:22–25 pars.). Possible echoes of Jesus' teaching also include 13:2 (cf. Matt. 17:20; 21:21). Yet clear use of Jesus' teaching seems strikingly minimal as an influence on the substance and presentation of Paul's ethics. More fundamental would seem to be Paul's Christology, in that he presents Christ both as the basis for unity and diversity in the community—"You are the body of Christ" (12:26)—and as the paradigm of self-giving and other-regard (10:33–11:1).

In an important rhetorical analysis of 1 Corinthians, Margaret Mitchell argues that the fundamental "thesis" of the letter is found in 1:10, in the appeal for ecclesial unity. Her analysis of the following sections of the letter as "proofs" in support of this central argument seems occasionally forced, but the notion that the letter is focused around this theme of community unity is well founded. Indeed, some of the language Paul uses, especially in the opening chapters, seems close to the language of ancient political discourse dealing with factionalism and rivalry. Others have pushed a political-ethical reading of 1 Corinthians further, arguing that Paul is seeking to strengthen the *ekklēsia* as an alternative society, standing in contrast and opposition to the imperial society ruled by Rome. David Horrell has argued that the metanorms of Paul's ethics, in 1 Corinthians and elsewhere, can be summarized as those of corporate solidarity and other-regard. Paul uses the ideas of the body of Christ, incorporation into Christ, and so on as a basis for community unity, but he equally stresses the need for this to be a diverse community. Even on some topics of ethical dispute, most notably concerning food offered to idols, he does not set out a ruling on the specific practice that is correct. Rather, he appeals for the practice of Christlike other-regard, which respects the interests and perspective of the other.

In terms of its relevance and contribution to contemporary ethical discourse, the appropriation of 1 Corinthians can operate at various levels. Christians study Paul's teaching on marriage and divorce, for example, to inform contemporary views on the subject. Some of the specific topics, such as food offered to idols, may be less directly relevant in Western contexts, but they are highly relevant in countries such as China and Indonesia, where Christians struggle to negotiate a stance regarding customs such as offerings to ancestors. On a broader level, Paul's way of doing ethics and the moral norms that inform this may be found instructive as a model for Christian ethics. The strongly christological basis to Paul's ethics means that he presents, in Alasdair MacIntyre's terms, a particular kind of tradition-specific and narratively founded ethics, while his concern to foster a corporate unity within which a (circumscribed) diversity of convictions and practices may be sustained bears some similarity to the central project of political liberalism.

Bibliography

Adams, E., and D. Horrell, eds. *Christianity at Corinth: The Quest for the Pauline Church.* Westminster John Knox, 2004.

Deming, W. *Paul on Marriage and Celibacy: The Hellenistic Background to 1 Corinthians 7.* SNTSMS 83. Cambridge University Press, 1995.

Furnish, V. "Belonging to Christ: A Paradigm for Ethics in First Corinthians." *Int* 44 (1990): 145–57.

Horrell, D. *Solidarity and Difference: A Contemporary Reading of Paul's Ethics.* T&T Clark, 2005.

Meeks, W. "The Polyphonic Ethics of the Apostle Paul." *ASCE* (1988): 17–29.

Mitchell, M. *Paul and the Rhetoric of Reconciliation: An Exegetical Investigation of the Language and Composition of 1 Corinthians.* HUT 28. Mohr Siebeck, 1991.

Rosner, B. *Paul, Scripture and Ethics: A Study of 1 Corinthians 5–7.* AGJU 22. Brill, 1994.

Wenham, D. *Paul: Follower of Jesus or Founder of Christianity?* Eerdmans, 1995.

◆ 2 Corinthians ◆

David J. Downs

The letter known as 2 Corinthians is not, in fact, the second letter that Paul sent to the Christian community in Corinth. It was preceded by at least two earlier epistles from the apostle to Corinth: one missive (unfortunately, no longer extant) mentioned in 1 Cor. 5:9; the other the canonical letter called "1 Corinthians." The text of 2 Corinthians itself gives some indication that it may consist of two (or more) originally separate epistles, for there is a marked shift in tone between chapters 1–9, which are largely conciliatory in nature, and chapters 10–13, which reflect a context of hostility and tension between the apostle and some opponents whom Paul somewhat sarcastically labels "super-apostles" (2 Cor. 11:5; 12:11). In its canonical form, however, 2 Corinthians offers a rich resource for reflection on the nature of Christian ministry and community.

One of Paul's major concerns in 2 Corinthians, and perhaps the point at which the letter raises the most questions for contemporary ethical reflection, is found in the apostle's attempt in chapters 8–9 to persuade the Corinthians to renew their support of the relief fund that Paul was organizing among the gentile churches of his mission for impoverished members of the Jewish Christian community in Jerusalem (see Rom. 15:25–32). Procedures for organizing this collection are explained in 1 Cor. 16:1–4, where Paul seems confident of the Corinthians' participation in the offering. In between the writing of 1 Corinthians and 2 Corinthians, however, Paul and the Corinthians had experienced no small conflict (see 2 Cor. 1:15–2:13), a clash (perhaps motivated by charges of financial impropriety leveled against Paul) that seems to have led the Corinthians to suspend their efforts to gather a collection for Jerusalem. There are indications in 2 Corinthians that Paul's opponents in Corinth seized on this controversy by charging Paul with financial impropriety (2 Cor. 11:7–15; 12:11–21).

Thus, 2 Cor. 8:1–9:15 is written with the goal of cautiously encouraging the Corinthians to resume their support of the relief fund for needy believers in Jerusalem. In this section Paul employs a striking variety of rhetorical appeals to accomplish this aim: (1) he emphasizes the example of the Macedonians, who have generously contributed to the fund in spite of their own deep poverty (8:1–6); (2) he highlights the paradigmatic grace (*charis*) of the incarnate Lord Jesus Christ, "who became poor for your sake, although he was rich, so that by his poverty you might become rich" (8:9); (3) he draws upon the principle of "equality" (*isotēs*) to promote a sharing of financial resources among believers in different economic and geographical locations (8:14); (4) he suggests that both he and the Corinthians will be shamed if believers come from Macedonia to Corinth and find the undertaking unfinished (9:1–5); (5) he paints an agricultural metaphor to suggest that giving to the collection is like sowing seed, a metaphor that emphasizes the generative activity of God in the act of human beneficence (9:6–10); and, finally, (6) he punctuates this appeal by indicating that true generosity results in thanksgiving and praise to God, the one from whom all benefactions ultimately originate (9:11–15). In his appeal Paul consistently underscores the point that the fulfillment of mutual obligations within the Christian community results in praise, not to human donors, as the dominant ideology of patronage in his cultural context would have suggested, but to God, the one from whom all benefactions come. Even the very human action of raising money for those in material need originates in "the surpassing grace of God" (*hē hyperballousa charis tou theou*) and will result in "thanks to God" (*charis tō theō*) (2 Cor. 9:14–15).

Paul therefore challenges the Corinthians to conceptualize their beneficence as an act of worship, offered in praise to God. In this profoundly theocentric vision of gift-giving within the community of faith, the willing generosity of the Corinthians is empowered by and patterned after the grace of God in Christ. Moreover, in appealing to the principle of financial equality between the Corinthians and impoverished believers in Jerusalem (8:13–15), Paul assumes that believers with more abundant resources will work to address the needs of those who require assistance, even as the Corinthians might someday require aid from Jerusalem (8:14).

Other motivations surely were behind Paul's efforts to organize a collection for Jerusalem, not the least of which was the apostle's goal of demonstrating an ecumenical solidarity between the gentile churches of his mission and the Christ-believing community in Jerusalem (cf. Rom. 15:25–32). Yet, to the extent that the contribution was aimed at meeting the very real financial needs of destitute believers in Jerusalem, readers today might ask themselves how individual and congregational resources can be used to support brothers and sisters in Christ who are experiencing economic distress. In a world of increasing disparity between the rich and poor—to say nothing of the extent to which globalization and technology have made these inequalities both manifest and also seemingly inescapable—the attempt to embody the kind of ecclesiological equality called for in 2 Cor. 8–9 is no easy task. Paul's own logic would seem to preclude the development of any kind of fixed rule for resource sharing (2 Cor. 8:8, 12; 9:5–7). Nonetheless, faithfulness to the message of 2 Corinthians will not allow those whose lives are shaped by the narrative of the incarnate Christ to stand by while massive inequality exists among churches. What is needed is not a law for giving but rather the empowering grace of the God who still stands behind all human generosity.

Bibliography

Cherian, J. "Toward a Commonwealth of Grace: A Plutocritical Reading of Grace and Equality in Second Corinthians 8:1–15." PhD diss., Princeton Theological Seminary, 2007.

Downs, D. J. *The Offering of the Gentiles: Paul's Collection for Jerusalem in Its Chronological, Cultural, and Cultic Contexts.* WUNT 2/248. Mohr Siebeck, 2008.

Wheeler, S. *Wealth as Peril and Obligation: The New Testament on Possessions.* Eerdmans, 1995, 73–89.

Young, F., and D. Ford. *Meaning and Truth in 2 Corinthians.* Eerdmans, 1988.

✦ Galatians ✦

Victor Paul Furnish

In this letter Paul expresses astonishment that certain unnamed teachers who seem to have insinuated themselves into his Galatian churches are persuading some members of those congregations to abandon the gospel that he had proclaimed to them. He is concerned, especially, that those gentile believers have been deceived into thinking that they must submit to various requirements of the Jewish law, including circumcision and the kosher table. The apostle seeks to refute this false teaching by asserting the divine origin of his law-free gospel and reminding the Galatians of its central affirmations.

Paul emphasizes that he proclaims Jesus Christ as the crucified Son of God (2:20–21; 3:1, 13–14), and that Christ's saving death has inaugurated a "new creation" (6:15) that believers experience as rectification ("justification" [2:16, 17, 21; 3:24; 5:4]) and freedom (2:4; 5:1, 13). Because "God shows no partiality" (2:6), this is "good news" for gentiles as well as for Jews (2:7–10; 3:28; 6:16).

What Paul means by the new creation, rectification, and freedom is expressed more concretely in a series of images. Believers are no longer enslaved to the "present evil age" (1:4), the law (3:23), the "elemental spirits of the world" (4:3), or their own desires (5:16–17). Having been "baptized into Christ," they are also "clothed" with him (3:27) and adopted as God's children (3:26; 4:1–3). They are therefore, even as gentiles, "Abraham's offspring, heirs according to the promise" (3:14–20, 29). Moreover, as "children of [God's] promise" (4:28), they have received God's Spirit (3:2, 5, 14; 4:6), by whom they are enabled to live out in the present the rectification already accomplished and to await with hope its ultimate fulfillment (5:5–6, 16–18, 22, 25; 6:8).

The explicit ethical appeals of this letter, which are concentrated in 5:13–6:10, are anticipated in the declaration that what matters most is not "circumcision" or "uncircumcision"—one's relationship to the law—but "faith made effective through love" (5:6 NRSV mg.). For Paul, faith is elicited by God's love as it has been revealed in the faithfulness of God's Son, "who loved . . . and gave himself" for others (2:20). And faith is expressed concretely as believers become agents of God's love in the world. Accordingly, the appeals in 5:13–6:10 highlight several ways in which the selfless love of Christ ought to be active in the lives of those who belong to him. Paul seems to be thinking especially of the perilous situation in the Galatian churches, where disputes about circumcision and other Jewish practices were turning Christian against Christian (5:15, 26 [note also, in 5:19–21, the inclusion of vices such as "strife," "quarrels," "dissensions," and "factions" in his listing of "the works of the flesh"]).

The introductory appeal (5:13) urges the Galatians not to use their freedom to serve their own interests (literally, "the flesh"), but, paradoxically, to bind themselves to one another "through love," as "slaves" are bound in service to their masters. Over against those who hold that gentile believers must adopt Jewish practices, Paul declares that the whole law is summed up in the one commandment to love the neighbor (5:14 [cf. "the law of Christ" in 6:2]). His summons to "live by the Spirit" (5:16–25) is also a call for the outworking of faith in love, for he regards love as the first and all-inclusive "fruit of the Spirit." No less important, his concluding appeal (6:10) to "work for the good of all" enlarges the field of love's service to include even those who stand outside the "family of faith."

Three significant convictions inform and support the ethical appeals in this letter. (1) What matters most is not one's adherence to religious rites and rules, but the "new creation" that God has inaugurated through Christ's death on the cross (6:14–15) and "faith made effective through love" (5:6). (2) Those who have been "baptized into Christ" understand that one's true identity is not contingent on religious, ethnic, social, or sexual status (3:27–28), but on one's standing before God and in Christ (e.g., 2:19–20). (3) Life before God and in Christ is simultaneously life in the Spirit, through whose empowering presence believers are guided in the ways of love (5:16–25). These same convictions, variously developed and expressed, are evident throughout all of Paul's letters.

Bibliography

Barclay, J. *Obeying the Truth: A Study of Paul's Ethics in Galatians*. SNTW. T&T Clark, 1988.

Hays, R. "Galatians." Pages 181–348 in *The New Interpreter's Bible*, vol. 11, ed. L. Keck. Abingdon, 2000.

Martyn, J. *Galatians*. AB 33A. Doubleday, 1997.

◆ Ephesians ◆

Jerry L. Sumney

Ephesians addresses a more general audience and a less specific situation than any of the undisputed Pauline Letters. By its time, arguments about the place of gentiles in the church had cooled, so the letter's emphasis on unity is less polemical than what we find in Galatians. The arguments in Ephesians remain so general that many see it as a kind of circular letter. Its emphasis on unity makes Ephesians a letter that focuses on innerecclesial relations.

This ecclesial focus dominates the ethical outlook of Ephesians. The constant theme within its exhortations is conduct in relation to fellow believers. When the letter calls readers to tell the truth to their "neighbors," the motivation is that "we are members of one another" (4:25). Ephesians does not attend to the effects that church members' lives have on outsiders. This letter ties proper ethics to proper teaching; living the Christian life helps one maintain correct doctrine (4:13–16). Ethical behavior lies at the heart of Christian existence; the believer's purpose is to do good works (2:10).

Most of the recommendations in Ephesians about Christian ethics are consistent with first-century cultural values. Among the few places where it differs are its recommendation of humility as a virtue (4:2) and its commendation of manual labor (4:28). The household code in Ephesians exemplifies its acceptance of cultural structures; it adopts the cultural expectations of first-century household life but gives them Christian groundings. (Ephesians may address households in which the head of the household is a believer, which sets it apart from those addressed in Colossians and 1 Peter.) Ephesians differs from the surrounding culture in the grounds that it proffers more than in the values that it promotes.

Still, Ephesians insists that the church remain distinct from the world. Succumbing to vices contradicts the believer's status as a participant in Christ (4:21). Believers must stop living as they did when they were "gentiles" or one of the "children of darkness" and must adopt a manner of life consistent with who God is and what God has done for them (4:17–18; 5:6–10). Thus, believers must forgive one another because God forgave them in Christ (4:32), and they must live in love because Christ loved them (5:2).

The emphasis in Ephesians on a distinctive manner of life promotes group solidarity by separating the church from the world. Perhaps Ephesians wants the church to differ from the world by actually living by the shared virtues and avoiding the acknowledged vices. This letter asserts that believers can live by higher standards because God enables them to do so. The number of times Ephesians calls believers saints ("holy ones") (1:2, 15, 18; 2:19; 3:8, 18; 4:12; 5:3; 6:18 [additional references to holiness appear in 1:4; 2:21; 5:27]) demonstrates the importance that it gives to fulfilling the demand to live righteously. Other Pauline Letters regularly call believers "saints," but none use this title as often as Ephesians does. Holy living is an essential element of Christian life for Ephesians.

The foundational admonition in Ephesians is "Be imitators of God, as beloved children" (5:1). Believers' lives should reflect who God is. Calls to imitate a god were not uncommon among first-century moralists. Further, this exhortation fits the grounding of ethics found in OT passages that urge the people to be holy because God is holy (e.g., Lev. 11:44; cf. 1 Pet. 1:16). Ephesians identifies Christ, particularly his self-giving death, as the clearest revelation of the character of God that believers are to imitate (4:32–5:2).

The partially realized eschatology of Ephesians comes to expression in its ethics. Believers put off the "old person" at conversion; now they must put on the "new person" that is appropriate to this new life. This "new person" is created by God in righteousness and purity (4:22–24). This notion coheres well with the initial and theme-setting exhortation of Eph. 4–6: "Live worthily of the calling with which you were called" (4:1). Living ethically is an essential element of a life that is consistent with what God in Christ has done for believers, whom God has made as "beloved children."

Bibliography

Best, E. *Essays on Ephesians.* T&T Clark, 1997.

Darko, D. *No Longer Living as the Gentiles: Differentiation and Shared Ethical Values in Ephesians 4.17–6.9.* LNTS 375. T&T Clark, 2008.

Lincoln, A. *Ephesians.* WBC 42. Thomas Nelson, 1990.

Malan, F. "Unity of Love in the Body of Christ: Identity, Ethics and Ethos in Ephesians." Pages 257–87 in *Identity, Ethics, and Ethos in the New Testament,* ed. J. van der Watt. BZNW 141. De Gruyter, 2006.

◆ Philippians ◆

Victor Paul Furnish

Writing from prison, Paul informs the Philippian Christians of his present circumstances and expectations, challenges them to be united and steadfast in their faith in the face of opposition from outsiders and dissension within their own community, and expresses appreciation for the financial assistance they had sent to him by way of Epaphroditus.

Standing at the theological and rhetorical center of Philippians is the "Christ hymn" (2:6–11), which tells the cosmic story of Christ's taking the form of a "slave" who is "obedient to the point of death" (2:6–8) and of God's subsequent exaltation of him to be the "Lord" of all creation (2:9–11). When Paul calls on his church to be of the "same mind" as Christ (2:5), he does not mean that it should take the earthly Jesus as its moral "role model." He is urging that its moral reasoning be informed and guided by the outlook that led Christ to "humble" himself and become "obedient" to God's will (2:6–8). The Christ-mindedness that Paul calls for as he introduces the hymn (2:5) is summed up in the immediately preceding appeal: "Let each of you look not to your own interests, but to the interests of others" (2:4 [cf. Rom. 15:2–3]).

This is a call for selfless, serving love (2:2 [cf. 1 Cor. 13:5]), which Paul had earlier named along with "knowledge and full insight" as critical for discerning "what is best" (1.9–10).

In addition to the definitive instance of Christ's self-giving, the letter offers several lesser examples of what it means to "look . . . to the interests of others": Timothy, "genuinely concerned for your welfare" (2:20–22); Epaphroditus, "your . . . minister to my need" (2:25, 29–30); and Paul himself, "Whatever gains I had, these I have come to regard as loss because of Christ" (3:4–11). The charge to "imitate" Paul and those who live according to his "example" (3:17) is, therefore, but another way of summoning the church to be of the "same mind" as Christ (so also 4:1, "stand firm in the Lord"). It is a summons to "know Christ and the power of his resurrection" as Paul knows these, by "sharing . . . his sufferings" and "becoming like him in his death" (3:10).

The general appeals for unity, selflessness, and steadfastness likely were prompted by several particular concerns that Paul had about the Philippians. One was the opposition that these believers were continuing to face from outsiders. The apostle declares that even though they are already citizens of heaven, where Christ reigns as Lord (3:20), for the time being they are also citizens of this world, with continuing responsibilities for its welfare. Despite the risks, it is not apart from society but within it that they are both called and empowered to live in a manner "worthy of the gospel" (1:27–2:18). Moreover, Paul does not hesitate to commend, where he can, moral qualities and actions that were widely affirmed in the Greco-Roman world (4:8; cf. 4:5a, where "everyone" includes nonbelievers).

Paul is concerned, further, about a dispute between two leading members of the congregation, Euodia and Syntyche (4:2–3). Their conflict must have been consequential, or Paul would not have singled it out for attention. With an implicit appeal to the selflessness of Christ (2:6–11), he urges these women to "be of the same mind in the Lord" (4:2) and then requests a respected third party to help effect their reconciliation (4:3).

This moral outlook is evident also in the way Paul expresses gratitude for the congregation's financial support (4:10–20). Departing from the usual practice, he does not accept their help as a gift that needs to be reciprocated. He describes it, rather, as "a fragrant offering, a sacrifice acceptable and pleasing to God" (4:18). The ancient social conventions of giving and receiving served to protect the interests of each party to the relationship. Paul, however, views the Philippians' gift differently: acting with the mind of Christ, they had looked not to their "own interests" but to the "interests of others" (cf. 2 Cor. 8–9).

Bibliography

Fee, G. *Paul's Letter to the Philippians*. NICNT. Eerdmans, 1995.

Fowl, S. *Philippians*. THNTC. Eerdmans, 2005.

Hooker, M. "Philippians." Pages 467–549 in *The New Interpreter's Bible*, vol. 11, ed. L. Keck. Abingdon, 2000.

Meeks, W. "The Man from Heaven in Paul's Letter to the Philippians." Pages 329–36 in *The Future of Early Christianity: Essays in Honor of Helmut Koester*, ed. B. Pearson et al. Fortress, 1991.

◆ Colossians ◆

Jerry L. Sumney

The Letter to the Colossians addresses a church troubled by teachers who argue that salvation is not secure without a visionary experience in which believers observe and participate in the angels' worship of God. They urge the Colossians to adopt a regime of rituals and practices that produce such experiences. In response, the letter assures its readers that those "in Christ" have all spiritual blessings and that no imitation of, or deference to, angels can enhance one's relationship with God.

Ethics is central to the message of Colossians. Near the beginning, the letter says that the purpose of receiving knowledge of God is to live a life worthy of God (1:9–10). This letter focuses on both the status that baptism confers and the demand to live in a particular way it imposes. The image of "putting off" the old way of life and "putting on" a new life conformed to Christ echoes baptismal language (3:8, 12). Thus, Colossians inseparably links the blessings received in baptism with ethical living. Proper living is not simply a consequence of receiving salvation; it is a gift that believers receive in baptism.

Colossians 3:1–4 defines "seeking the things above" as ethical living. This introduction to a section on ethics tells believers that they "have been raised with Christ." Here, being raised with Christ does not signal exaltation but rather indicates that believers must pattern their lives after Christ because God has given them new life in him. Therefore, all aspects of life should conform to being in Christ.

Colossians' explication of this new life is consistent with some elements of first-century ethical thought but opposes other elements of it. Many contemporaneous moralists condemned most of the vices listed in 3:8. Some of the virtues mentioned in 3:12 (particularly humility), however, run counter to cultural values. Colossians evaluates all ethical values by whether they are consistent with being "in Christ."

The household code of 3:18 4:1 gives direct instructions to wives and husbands, children and parents, slaves and owners. Similar registers of instructions appear in Ephesians, 1 Timothy, Titus, and 1 Peter. The concerns reflected in them go back to Aristotle's comments on household management (*Pol.* 1.3), but probably there was no precise literary form that these tables imitate.

The household code of Colossians is problematic because its apparent support of slavery and hierarchy within marriage seems to violate its previous ethical instructions. Unlike most moralists of the first century, the author of Colossians assumes that men and women in Christ should adopt the same virtues. Furthermore, in 3:11 the author proclaims that status markers make no difference in the church, but the code seems to reestablish them. The solution to this tension lies in recognizing the first-century church's position in relation to the broader culture. This code addresses wives, children, and slaves in households that have unbelievers as their heads. In such circumstances these subordinates had no choice but to fulfill their expected roles. All Colossians can do is redefine the meaning of their submission in ways that point to the incongruity between this ordering of relations and life in Christ. For example, wives are to submit "as is fitting in the Lord" (3:18). This phrase redefines submission so that it is proper for everyone, not just wives (if we take 3:11 seriously). This reading gains support from 3:19, which tells husbands not to be embittered toward their wives (the NRSV translation "never treat them harshly" is incorrect). Similarly, slaves are designated as heirs, and masters are told that they are slaves. Such statements counter the code's apparent call for conformity to first-century expectations. Thus, it enjoins those required to conform to do so but also to know that their forced subordination does not reflect God's will.

Colossians' treatment of ethics suggests that believers should look to the identity that they have been granted in Christ and the character of God for criteria to evaluate all the values, structures, and expectations of their culture.

Bibliography

Bevere, A. *Sharing in the Inheritance: Identity and the Moral Life in Colossians.* JSNTSup 226. Sheffield Academic Press, 2003.

Meeks, W. "'To Walk Worthily of the Lord': Moral Formation in the Pauline School Exemplified by the Letter to Colossians." Pages 37–58 in *Hermes and Athena: Biblical Exegesis and Philosophical Theology*, ed. E. Stump and T. Flint. University of Notre Dame Press, 1993.

Standhartinger, A. "The Epistle to the Congregation in Colossae and the Invention of the 'Household Code.'" Pages 88–121 in *A Feminist Companion to the Deutero-Pauline Epistles*, ed. A.-J. Levine and M. Blickenstaff. FCNTECW 7. T&T Clark, 2003.

Sumney, J. *Colossians*. NTL. Westminster, 2008.

✦ 1–2 Thessalonians ✦

Jerry L. Sumney

The letters of 1–2 Thessalonians address rather different circumstances and take rather different approaches to ethics. The primary occasion of 1 Thessalonians is Timothy's report to Paul that the churches in that city are remaining faithful despite persecutions and some confusion about what happens to believers who die before the second coming of Christ. Paul responds by interpreting their persecution as a sign of their faithfulness and by assuring them that the dead will participate fully in the resurrection. In 2 Thessalonians Paul seeks to combat an overrealized eschatology that claims that some Christians have already experienced a second coming that gives the participants spiritual superiority. This has led some who make this claim to quit their jobs and demand pay from the congregation for their work within the church. This letter argues that the second coming remains a future event, and that Christians must live their lives in the light of its judgment.

1 Thessalonians

Paul's answer to the Thessalonians' questions about persecution initiates his discussion of ethics in this letter. He asserts that God's people historically have experienced persecution, and that his readers have adopted a faithful manner of life in imitation of those earlier people of God. Paul explicates the proper manner of life more by way of examples than specific instruction. He says that they have become imitators of him, Christ, earlier believers, and perhaps the prophets, and he exhorts them to follow such examples. Then he notes that they have become examples to others. Imitation is a significant element of the way ethics is taught and encouraged in 1 Thessalonians.

Paul defines God's will for believers as sanctification, being made holy (4:3, 7). One motivation he identifies for living a holy life is that the believer might be found guiltless at judgment. Indeed, the letter's most concentrated section on ethics leads into Paul's discussion of eschatology. He says that it is necessary for believers to live in a way that pleases God, and that such behavior distinguishes them from unbelievers.

However, this ethic does not remove believers from the world. Instead, they are to be concerned about how unbelievers perceive them (4:11–12; 5:15). They should exemplify the virtues of self-sufficiency and peacefulness. In this way, living properly pleases God and ameliorates, perhaps even invites in, their neighbors.

More often, though, 1 Thessalonians emphasizes innerchurch relations. Paul's ministry provides an example for the Thessalonians because his life among them was not only honest but also gentle and self-giving (2:1–12). The concluding exhortations also focus on relations among church members, how they are to treat leaders, the disorderly, and the weak. Thus, the ethic of this letter is strongly inner-directed.

Although 1 Thessalonians is focused on two problems that are not directly ethical, ethics plays a large role in the letter. How one lives is a central element in its teaching about persecution and eschatology. There is little explicit instruction about particular behaviors, but proper living is seen as a central part of what it means to be a believer. Not only will behavior be important at judgment but also it is a part of God's will for them. Since proper living includes both innerchurch relations and relations with outsiders, the whole of the believer's life is to be formed by imitation of Christ.

2 Thessalonians

Perhaps it is the continuing disadvantage or persecution experienced by the Thessalonians that leads 2 Thessalonians to emphasize the judgment and punishment coming on unbelievers. Retribution for those troubling the church is a central theme of the thanksgiving and other parts of this letter. It asserts that judgment against such people has already begun because they are the people who will believe the false wonders that Satan empowers (2:8–12).

Conversely, 2 Thessalonians gives being found not guilty at judgment a central place in motivating its readers to live ethically. Still, God's call and love empower believers to live for God. Indeed, God's call includes the expectation that the believer will live a sanctified/holy life (2:13–14). The lives of Paul and other faithful leaders exemplify the holy living believers are to imitate (3:6–7), but prior apostolic instruction is the basis for determining what constitutes ethical living. Christians who fail to live by the expected standards, however, are not relegated to the ranks of the unbelievers destined for destruction. Such errant believers remain part of the family of believers, and they must be set apart from the community but not treated as enemies. Rather, the church is to nurture their return to full fellowship (3:14–15). Like other Pauline Letters, 2 Thessalonians links ethical living and doing good works with correct teaching; only those who believe the right doctrine will be able to live ethically (2:15–17).

The conduct of the "disorderly" (the "idle" of 3:6–15) flows from their overrealized eschatology. Asserting that their experience of a spiritual coming of Christ gives them superior spiritual blessings and abilities, they quit their jobs, impose themselves as ministers on this church, and demand salaries. This letter rejects their eschatology and understanding of spirituality by telling the church not to support them. Proper conduct for ministers follows the apostolic example of giving of oneself for the good of the church, and it does not include demanding deference and pay.

The letter of 2 Thessalonians contains few instructions about what constitutes proper living, expecting its readers to know what behavior the apostolic tradition requires. It focuses more on assessment at judgment than on motivations based on believers' new identity as God's children or one's place in Christ. The latter kinds of motivations are not absent from 2 Thessalonians, but they do play a much smaller role than in other Pauline Letters.

Bibliography

Donfried, K. *Paul, Thessalonica, and Early Christianity*. Eerdmans, 2002.

Furnish, V. *1 Thessalonians, 2 Thessalonians*. ANTC. Abingdon, 2007.

Getty, M. "The Imitation of Paul in the Letters to the Thessalonians." Pages 277–83 in *The Thessalonian Correspondence*, ed. R. Collins. BETL 87. Leuven University Press, 1990.

Malherbe, A. *Paul and the Thessalonians: The Philosophic Tradition of Pastoral Care*. Fortress, 1987.

Still, T. *Conflict at Thessalonica: A Pauline Church and Its Neighbours*. JSNTSup 183. Sheffield Academic Press, 1999.

◆ 1–2 Timothy ◆

David J. Downs

Although 1 Timothy and 2 Timothy typically are grouped, along with Titus, as part of a single corpus known as the Pastoral Epistles, each document

addresses a particular situation. Therefore, the moral issues dealt with and
the potential contribution of each letter to contemporary ethical reflection
differ due to the diverse rhetorical aims of each composition. Here, the two
letters to Timothy will be treated separately. Although both letters often are
considered by most scholars to be pseudonymous writings, the implied author
of the texts is Paul, whether or not he is the real author.

1 Timothy

The first letter of Paul to Timothy is predominantly concerned with the threat
of opponents who are advocating "different doctrine" (1:3). These false teachers, two of whom are identified by name in 1:20, are accused of devoting themselves to "myths and endless genealogies" (1:4), of forbidding marriage and
demanding abstinence from certain foods (4:3), and of triggering controversy
within the congregation that leads to envy, dissension, slander, suspicion, and
division (6:3–5).

In light of this challenge, Paul offers his "loyal child in the faith" (1:2) instruction regarding church life (2:1–3:16; 5:1–6:2) and teaching on Timothy's
own duties as a believer and leader (4:1–16; 6:3–21). Some of the ecclesiological
directives in 1 Timothy draw on conventional Hellenistic ethical discourse (cf.
the qualities for church leadership in 3:1–12 with Onasander, *Strat.* 1). Yet
often Paul's ethical instructions are given explicit theological grounding. For
example, the critique of those who imagine that "there is great gain in godliness" is rooted in the understanding that those who brought nothing into the
world will take nothing out of it (6:6–7). Therefore, the rich in the present age
should share generously with others (6:17–19). Similarly, the rejection of the
ascetic practices of the opponents is warranted by a theology of the goodness
of creation (4:4). Whereas the opponents insist on an ethical asceticism that
takes believers away from the world, Paul calls Timothy, and by extension all
believers, to a deep engagement with the world.

This coherence between the church and the world in 1 Timothy is highlighted by the metaphor of the *ekklēsia* as the "household of God" (3:15).
The structures of the household become the structures of the church (5:1–6:2).
On the one hand, this metaphor runs the risk of encouraging the church
simply to accept or endorse the patriarchal values of the Greco-Roman
household. This seems to be the case regarding the instructions given to
men and women in the context of prayer and worship in 2:8–15, a text in
which the restrictions on the role of women in worship stand in some tension with the other Pauline Letters (e.g., Rom. 16:7; 1 Cor. 11:2–16; Gal.

3:28; but cf. 1 Cor. 14:33–36). On the other hand, 1 Timothy consistently reflects a desire to protect and maximize the effectiveness of the church's witness in the world (e.g., 2:1–7). For those tempted to become frustrated with the somewhat conservative social ethic represented in 1 Timothy, perhaps recognition that this ethic is rooted in a missional concern to guard the church's public witness to the gospel will temper discontent with the perspective articulated in the letter.

2 Timothy

The letter of 2 Timothy is a testamentary epistle from the apostle Paul to his "beloved child" Timothy (1:2). Paul is in prison at the time of the letter's composition (1:8, 15–18), quite likely facing the prospect of his death (4:6–8). An important theme in 2 Timothy is that of Paul's exhortation to his younger associate to remain faithful to the testimony about the Lord at a time when Timothy seems tempted to be shamed by the gospel. Timothy's wavering commitment seems to be due, at least in part, to perceptions about Paul's own weakness as a prisoner of Christ (1:6–2:7) and to the threat of conflict from within the church (1:15–16; 2:14–26; 3:1–9, 13; 4:3–5). Thus, Paul's testament aims at encouraging and challenging Timothy in the face of the younger man's shame and in response to the danger of false teaching.

One way that Paul accomplishes his goal is by highlighting examples of faithful witness. These examples include the sincere faith of Timothy's grandmother and mother (1:3–5; 3:14); the model of Paul's own suffering as a prisoner for the Lord (1:8–14; 2:9; 3:10–12; 4:6–8); the willing service of Onesiphorus, who was not ashamed of Paul's chains (1:15–18); the images of the solider, athlete, and farmer that demonstrate persistent commitment in the pursuit of a specific goal (2:3–6); and the paradigm of Christ's own vicarious suffering (2:11). Negatively, Hymenaeus and Philetus are singled out as those who have "swerved from the truth by claiming that the resurrection has already taken place" (2:18; cf. 3:8). Thus, Paul's call for Timothy to remain steadfast in his commitment to the gospel is warranted by a series of models of faithful commitment. Perhaps the most important example is found in Christ's own faithfulness on behalf of those who have died and will live with him (2:8–13). If the moral requirements in 1 Timothy reflect a context of (relatively) positive relations between church and world, 2 Timothy speaks more directly to believers facing marginalization and hostility because of their adherence to the gospel. In 2 Timothy, as in other texts in the NT, cruciform ethics are shaped by the experience of suffering.

Bibliography

Aageson, J. *Paul, the Pastoral Epistles, and the Early Church*. Hendrickson, 2008.

De Villiers, P. "Heroes at Home: Identity, Ethos, and Ethics in 1 Timothy within the Context of the Pastoral Epistles." Pages 357–86 in *Identity, Ethics, and Ethos in the New Testament*, ed. J. van der Watt and F. Malan. BZNW 141. De Gruyter, 2006.

Scholer, D. "1 Timothy 2.9–15 and the Place of Women in the Church's Ministry." Pages 98–121 in *A Feminist Companion to the Deutero-Pauline Epistles*, ed. A.-J. Levine and M. Blickenstaff. FCNTECW 7. T&T Clark, 2003.

Young, F. *The Theology of the Pastoral Letters*. NTT. Cambridge University Press, 1994, 24–46.

◆ Titus ◆

David J. Downs

The Letter to Titus, ostensibly written by the apostle Paul to a younger ministry associate in Crete, focuses on the necessity of sound teaching and virtuous living in light of the threat of false instruction within the Christian community. The author is alarmed about "rebellious people, idle talkers and deceivers," particularly those of a group that he labels "the circumcision" (1:10). It is likely that the opponents of the author, like those addressed in Galatians, were encouraging gentile believers to abide by the Torah (1:13–15; 3:9).

Unlike Paul in Galatians, however, the author of Titus does not engage in a sustained theological and hermeneutical debate with the views of his opponents. Instead, the false teachers are condemned (1:15–16; 3:9), and Titus is encouraged to teach "sound doctrine" (2:1) and to exhort various groups within the churches to live respectable lives. Qualifications for elders (1:6) and overseers (1:7–9) are articulated in terms that emphasize a leader's honorable character in domestic, interpersonal, and ecclesiastical settings. Similarly, the author adapts the literary form of "household code" in order to urge older men (2:2), older women (2:3–5), younger men (2:6–8), and slaves (2:9–10) to virtuous living that will not compromise Christian witness in the world. Moreover, the entire Christian community is exhorted "to be subject to rulers and authorities, to be obedient, to be ready for every good work, to speak evil of no one, to avoid quarrelling, to be gentle, and to show every courtesy to everyone" (3:1–2). This appeal for obedience to secular authorities corresponds to other NT texts that counsel subordination to political rulers as an aspect of Christian mission (cf. Rom. 13:1–7; 1 Pet. 2:12–17). Yet while these instructions in Titus are framed in terms that largely correspond to contemporary

Greco-Roman virtues, the paraenesis is also rooted in the author's insistence that the grace of God and eschatological expectation of the future appearance of Jesus lead believers to "good deeds" (2:11–14; 3:3–8).

That Titus is viewed by a majority of NT scholars as a pseudonymous composition, written in Paul's name after the apostle's death, raises moral questions related to its interpretation for some. If the document perpetuates a deception (although a case can be made that Titus is not pseudonymous), does this literary fiction violate the claims of truth and trustworthiness made within the text itself (1:1, 12–13; 3:8)? The answer to this question rests in part on whether the practice of pseudonymity in antiquity was an accepted literary device. Some who concede the pseudonymous nature of Titus locate the practice not in deception but rather in the actualization of an earlier authoritative tradition in a new setting, with similar examples occurring in Jewish apocalyptic, prophetic, and wisdom traditions (e.g., Deutero-Isaiah, *Psalms of Solomon*).

Bibliography

Donelson, L. *Pseudepigraphy and Ethical Argument in the Pastoral Epistles*. HUT 22. Mohr Siebeck, 1986.

Meade, D. *Pseudonymity and Canon: An Investigation into the Relationship of Authorship and Authority in Jewish and Earliest Christian Tradition*. WUNT 39. Mohr Siebeck, 1986.

Young, F. *The Theology of the Pastoral Letters*. NTT. Cambridge University Press, 1994, 24–46.

◆ Philemon ◆
Victor Paul Furnish

Philemon is both the shortest of Paul's letters and the only one in which, primarily, just one person is addressed. Philemon was the patron of a house church (probably in Colossae), a man well known by Paul, and perhaps one of the apostle's own converts (v. 19). The letter, written from prison in an unnamed location, is an appeal on behalf of Philemon's slave Onesimus, who has wronged his master in some unspecified way. There is no evidence to support the traditional view that he was a fugitive from Philemon's household who subsequently was confined in the same prison from which Paul was writing. Yet somehow the two were in touch during the apostle's imprisonment, and he converted Onesimus to the gospel (v. 10).

There is no deliberate theological exposition or argumentation in this letter, and the theological grounding of the appeal to Philemon must be largely inferred. The inferences, however, are not difficult to draw. Paul addresses Philemon, first of all, not as the master of Onesimus but as his (the apostle's) friend and co-worker (v. 1), the patron of a house church (v. 2), and a person who has shown "love for all the saints" and "faith toward the Lord Jesus" (v. 5; cf. v. 7). When, therefore, Paul goes on to say that his appeal to Philemon is made "on the basis of love" (v. 9), presumably he is thinking both of God's love that elicits faith and the love through which that faith is actualized in the lives of believers (see Gal. 5:6 NRSV mg.), like Philemon himself.

It is specifically the circulation of love within the believing community (the *koinōnia* of faith [v. 6]) that is on view here. Throughout, Paul uses kinship terms to describe the relationships that bind the members of this community together: Paul's conversion of Onesimus makes the apostle his "father" and the convert a "son" (v. 10); Timothy is "the brother" (v. 1) and Apphia is "the sister" (v. 2); Philemon is not only Paul's "beloved friend," "co-worker," and "partner [*koinōnos*]" (vv. 1, 17) but also his "brother" (vv. 7, 20); and Paul hopes that Philemon will regard Onesimus as a "beloved brother," even as he himself does (v. 16). At several important points in the letter the phrases "in Christ" (vv. 8, 20), "in the Lord" (vv. 16, 20), and "in Christ Jesus" (v. 23) identify the sphere within which this whole network of relationships exists and is sustained.

The content of Paul's appeal for Onesimus (vv. 9–10) is not provided in the form of a directive until v. 17: "So if you [Philemon] consider me your partner, welcome him as you would welcome me." The convert, Onesimus, is to be accepted as a partner in the faith, "no longer as a slave" but as a "beloved brother," both in the workaday world and in the community of faith ("both in the flesh and in the Lord") (v. 16). Above all, the apostle wants to bring about reconciliation between these men, and he well understands that this will require a complete transformation of their relationship, even if their legal relationship as slave and master remains unchanged. But also, Paul strongly hints that when Philemon has accepted Onesimus as a Christian brother, he should allow him to resume his ministry, now on Philemon's behalf, with the imprisoned apostle (v. 13).

Paul writes with the authority of an apostle; he is "bold enough in Christ to command" (v. 8), and he expects Philemon's "obedience" (v. 21). Yet, his appeal is not based on this authority. He neither confronts Philemon with apostolic demands nor invokes the teaching of Jesus or the words of Scripture about mercy and compassion. He bases his appeal, rather, on the love that is constitutive of Christian community, through which its members are partners "in Christ" and brothers and sisters in the family of faith. Because reconciliation cannot be coerced, Paul leaves it to Philemon himself to determine what "good" he is called to do "for Christ" in the case of Onesimus.

In this letter one sees the apostle engaged in a "ministry of reconciliation" (see 2 Cor. 5:18). Although the parties most directly involved are a master and his slave, slavery itself is not Paul's subject. It is doubtful whether he or any other first-century Christian could have envisioned a political order without the institution of slavery, for it was one of the foundations of the social and economic stability of the Roman Empire (hence the instructions to masters and slaves in Eph. 6:5–9; Col. 3:22–4:1; cf. 1 Pet. 2:18–25). Moreover, even if Christians could have envisioned the abolition of slavery, they would have been powerless to bring it about. Thus, although the apostle may be hinting that Onesimus deserves manumission ("knowing that you will do even more than I say" [v. 21]), he remains silent on the injustice of slavery as an institution. This is also true when, elsewhere, he counsels slaves to gain their freedom if they have the opportunity (see 1 Cor. 7:21 NRSV mg.).

Nonetheless, for Paul, the institution of slavery belongs to the old age that is "passing away" (1 Cor. 7:31), for in God's "new creation," already inaugurated in Christ (2 Cor. 5:17), "there is no longer slave or free" because all are one in Christ (Gal. 3:27–28; cf. 1 Cor. 12:13; Col. 3:11). Paul's appeal to Philemon is, in effect, a summons to allow this new reality to work its transforming power in his relationship with Onesimus.

Bibliography

de Vos, C. "Once a Slave, Always a Slave? Slavery, Manumission and Relational Patterns in Paul's Letter to Philemon." *JSNT* 82 (2001): 89–105.

du Plessis, I. "How Christians Can Survive in a Hostile Social-economic Environment: Paul's Mind Concerning Difficult Social Conditions in the Letter to Philemon." Pages 387–413 in *Identity, Ethics, and Ethos in the New Testament*, ed. J. van der Watt. BZNW 141. De Gruyter, 2006.

Osiek, C. *Philippians, Philemon*. ANTC. Abingdon, 2000, 133–46.

4

‡‡‡

CATHOLIC EPISTLES AND REVELATION

♦ Hebrews ♦

David A. deSilva

The Epistle to the Hebrews is an anonymous sermon written by a member of the Pauline missionary team (as the author's acquaintance with Timothy suggests [13:23]). Since the author speaks of the Levitical sacrifices continuing to be offered in the present (9:9; 10:2), he probably wrote prior to the destruction of the Jerusalem temple in 70 CE. He addresses a congregation composed of both gentile Christians, for whom instruction in monotheism and the Jewish apocalyptic worldview would have been necessary (6:1–3), and Jewish Christians, with whom the author obviously shares deep roots in the Scriptures. These Christians previously suffered significant rejection at the hands of their neighbors (10:32–34), but some appear now to be in danger of drifting away from their formerly bold stance (2:1–2; 3:12–13; 4:1, 11; 10:24–27, 35–36), perhaps longing once again for some measure of acceptance by their non-Christian peers (the "fleeting pleasures of sin" [11:25]).

The chief ethical contribution of the sermon is the context that the author invokes for making ethical choices: the experience of God's generosity and kindness through Jesus Christ and the concomitant obligation to respond with gratitude in the form of witness, honor, and service (13:15–16). The ideals of the virtuous receiving and returning of favors taught by Greek and Roman ethicists are brought to bear on Christian discipleship, calling the audience not to take God's grace for granted, but to make their choices and lifestyle a consistent witness to their appreciation for God's favor. God's gifts call for appropriate response (6:4–8; 12:28) even when costly, since Jesus' display of favor on their behalf was costly in the extreme (13:12–14). Acts of service and encouragement offered to other members of the community (6:9–10; 10:24–25) are important responses. Choices that reflect a low estimation of Christ's death, most notably allowing one's desire for acceptance within non-Christian society to mute one's Christian witness and drawing back from investing oneself in the lives of fellow Christians, reflect a failure to respond nobly and gratefully (10:23–34). The author has in mind a particular challenge facing the congregation, but the canonical status of his sermon holds this question before disciples in all situations: what is the course of action that will most fully witness to my appreciation for God's favor, and offer the return that would be most pleasing to God (11:6; 12:28; 13:20–21) and most in keeping with the purposes inherent in redemption, as informed by the Judeo-Christian tradition? He urges his audience to replace their desire for "more" (which threatens their ethical integrity) with contentment and confidence in God's ongoing help (13:5–6)—an exhortation that remains a potent challenge to materialist societies.

Fear of divine judgment and retribution, such as would fall on the ungrateful or disloyal, is here an appropriate motivation for ethical decision (2:1–2; 6:4–8; 10:26–31; 12:25–29; 13:4). Such fear helps liberate disciples from the fear of death (2:14–15), which warps and limits ethical choice. Hardships incurred as a result of virtuous action or refusal to violate the bond of gratitude toward God are redeemed by the author as the crucible for character formation (5:8–9; 12:4–11).

The author is very much aware of the social dimension of ethical choice. Those whose approval we seek and whose censure we long to avoid directly influence the ethical decisions we make. The author seeks to exclude concern for one's estimation in the eyes of people not committed to the Christian way of life as a motivation for choice. This is prominent in the examples he praises in 10:32–34; 11:8–16, 24–27, 35–38; 12:1–3. Instead, he directs attention to the company of those who have fulfilled God's just requirements well in their lives—the praiseworthy heroes of the tradition and, above all, Jesus (12:1–2)—as those whose applause is worth seeking. He also encourages mutual investment and accountability in order to provide essential support for empowering individual disciples to make appropriate, often costly, ethical decisions (3:12–13; 5:11–6:1; 10:34; 12:15–16; 13:1–3).

The author is best known for his commendation of faith as an ethical virtue that guides disciples' actions (11:1–12:3). Faith acts with a view to long-term gain, even at the cost of short-term pain. Faith also entails courageous commitment (3:7–4:11; 10:36–39). Faith thus combines the cardinal virtues of wisdom and courage. Faith responds with trust and obedience to the divine word, with a view to attaining the divine promises, and so becomes productive of the other ethical virtues.

Bibliography

Attridge, H. *Hebrews*. Hermeneia. Fortress, 1989.

Croy, N. *Endurance in Suffering: Hebrews 12:1–13 in Its Rhetorical, Religious, and Philosophical Context*. SNTSMS 98. Cambridge University Press, 1998.

deSilva, D. *Despising Shame: The Social Function of the Rhetoric of Honor and Dishonor in the Epistle to the Hebrews*. SBLDS 152. Scholars Press, 1995.

———. *Perseverance in Gratitude: A Socio-Rhetorical Commentary on the Epistle "to the Hebrews."* Eerdmans, 2000.

Johnson, L. *Hebrews*. NTL. Westminster John Knox, 2006.

Koester, C. *Hebrews*. AB 36. Doubleday, 2001.

Witherington, B., III. *Letters and Homilies for Jewish Christians: A Socio-Rhetorical Commentary on Hebrews, James and Jude*. InterVarsity, 2007.

✦ James ✦

David Hutchinson Edgar

James is widely recognized as a text in which ethical exhortation receives greater prominence than more abstract reflection on doctrinal matters. There is no scholarly consensus as to whether the letter should be seen as deriving from James, the brother of Jesus and leader of the early Jerusalem church, or as a pseudonymous work from the latter part of the first century.

The opening verses introduce the key theme of undivided commitment to God in all circumstances. Such faithful commitment goes hand in hand with a God-given wisdom that is characteristic of life lived in harmony with the requirements of God's order of the universe (1:5–8; 3:13–18).

The demands of God's will for humankind are expressed by a variety of terms, including "the word of truth" (1:18), "the implanted word" (1:21), "the perfect law of liberty" (1:25; 2:12), and "the royal law according to the scripture" (2:8). The use of legal terminology to express God's will indicates a positive appropriation of the Jewish sense of law as expressing God's order. It seems likely, however, that such references are colored by an early Christian perspective influenced by the traditions of the sayings of Jesus, given a number of close parallels between the language and concerns of James and of the sayings of Jesus in the Gospels (e.g., Jas. 1:5 and Matt. 7:7; Luke 11:9; Jas. 1:9–10; 4:10 and Matt. 23:12; Luke 14:11; Jas. 1:17 and Matt. 7:11; Jas. 2:5 and Luke 6:20; Jas. 3:1 and Matt. 12:36–37; Jas. 5:1 and Luke 6:24–25; Jas. 5:2 and Matt. 6:19–20; Jas. 5:12 and Matt. 5:34).

The requirement for unqualified dependence on God embraces all aspects of human life. In three central discursive sections of the text, human attitudes and judgment (2:1–13), actions (2:14–26), and speech (3:1–12) are held up for scrutiny, and real or potential shortcomings in the addressees' conduct are exposed against the standard of faithful commitment to God (2:1, 5–6, 14–17).

The sense of dependence on God is consolidated by a strong conviction of the effectiveness of faithful prayer (1:5–8; 5:13–18), together with the portrayal of God as one whose inherent character is to give (1:5, 17–18). God's benefactions themselves appear to be part of that relationship of committed dependence on the part of believers: the one who doubts or who asks with dubious motives will not receive (1:6–8; 4:3).

A strong element of dualism informs the ethical exhortations of James, typified by the contrast between friendship with the world and friendship with God (4:4); the readers are urged to resist the devil (4:7), and, humbly accepting God's complete sovereignty, they will receive God's reward. An eschatological dimension to such admonitions seems clear (2:5; 5:7–11), but the text's concerns should also be seen as relating to the immediate circumstances of its readers.

In particular, the context of trials or testing of faith is invoked in 1:2–4, 12–15. Such testing may well relate to the adverse socioeconomic situations elicited by the author a number of times in the letter (1:9–11, 27; 2:2–7, 15–16; 5:4). The contrast between the negative portrayal of the rich and the sense of God's favor to the poor and humble is striking. In a world of scarce resources, where a high degree of social and economic control was exercised through the relationship between patron and client, the negative view of the rich may be closely related to the imperative of undivided commitment to God: God, not any agent of the transient, human, earthly order, is the one who gives unstintingly and who should be relied on in all circumstances. Human conduct should involve solidarity with the victims of the oppressive and ungodly structures of the present earthly order (1:27; 2:1–9, 14–17) and a renunciation of its values and status symbols (3:13–18; 4:13–5:6).

The ethical message of James is uncompromising. The faith of the Christian inevitably carries the demand of undivided commitment to God in lives lived in accordance with God's will. The importance of prayer in acknowledging God's sovereignty and provision is highlighted, as is the call to solidarity with those burdened by the oppressive structures of the human social order.

Bibliography

Bauckham, R. *James: Wisdom of James, Disciple of Jesus the Sage*. NTR. Routledge, 1999.

Hartin, P. *A Spirituality of Perfection: Faith in Action in the Letter of James*. Liturgical Press, 1999.

Hutchinson Edgar, D. *Has God Not Chosen the Poor? The Social Setting of the Epistle of James*. JSNTSup 206. Sheffield Academic Press, 2001.

Jackson-McCabe, M. *Logos and Law in the Letter of James: The Law of Nature, the Law of Moses, and the Law of Freedom*. NovTSup 100. Brill, 2001.

Wachob, W. *The Voice of Jesus in the Social Rhetoric of James*. SNTSMS 106. Cambridge University Press, 2000.

◆ 1 Peter ◆

J. de Waal Dryden

The Epistle of 1 Peter presents a banquet of ethical material, with numerous ethical admonitions and injunctions concerning issues such as household codes, Christian identity and lifestyle in a pagan society, and deference to the state. But it would be a mistake to see this epistle as simply an inchoate reservoir of ethical teachings. In fact, these ethical materials are signposts that lead to recognizing a coherent intentionality in the epistle. First Peter is an example of wisdom literature. It is written to shape the character of beleaguered Christian communities in northern Asia Minor, to encourage practical dependence on God, displaying his holy and gracious character through deepening expressions of love in the community and sustaining moral integrity toward those outside.

First Peter is an example of a paraenetic epistle, a prominent form of wisdom literature in the Greco-Roman philosophical schools. As an integrated piece of wisdom, it combines the ethical materials mentioned above with other themes that provide an intellectual context and affective motivations for considered moral action. For example, the typical wisdom theme of the "two ways" is prominent in 1 Peter, especially as related to the dichotomy of preconversion life (denigrated as "futile" in 1:18) and postconversion life (characterized by purity, love, obedience, and incorruptibility in 1:14–23). In addition, the Christology of the epistle is almost exclusively devoted to portraying Jesus as an exemplar of one who, out of reverent devotion to God, courageously maintained his moral integrity in the face of unjust suffering (2:21–25). This shaping of Christology to contextualize and motivate moral action is typical of the theology of the epistle as a whole, which is organized according to pragmatic more than systematic concerns. Theology serves the purpose of wisdom—to orient communal life toward a world where a righteous "way of life" (*anastrophē*) is comprehensible, laudable, and desirable. Whether in Christology, eschatology (1:13), or the new birth (1:3), doctrinal teaching moves immediately to practical implication and serves the paraenetic wisdom agenda of shaping communal life in its concreteness.

First Peter is addressed to Christian churches under threat, ostracized for their distinct beliefs and lifestyle and for their lack of conformity to normative social practices. Experiencing the pain of social rejection and alienation, they are simultaneously tempted toward conformity, isolation, and retaliation. It is in this context that the author encourages these churches to retain their Christian identity and to continue to "do good." To many this call to do good has seemed a strange response to persecution, but for our author, the greatest challenge of suffering is not despondency but vice. The moral challenges of suffering, the corruption of character and corporate life, the temptations to vengeance, isolation, and selfishness are the main targets that the author has in view in writing to these careworn Anatolian churches. So it is not surprising that from the start (1:6) the author interprets their persecutions through the image of a refining fire (another archetypal wisdom theme). In this way, sufferings have the potential of becoming a means of salvation (1:9), producing a strengthened faith that is worth more than gold (1:7). This process, however, is not automatic. Suffering has the power to refine character only when it is met with actions that reflect both the holiness and hospitality of God.

Social persecution is a dangerous challenge to the corporate identity and distinctive lifestyle of these Christian communities. The defining and retention of corporate identity is thus a key component in the author's agenda. Incorporating images from the OT, the author defines corporate identity in terms of the electing love of God. They are a people chosen by God, a people defined by the fact that they have been shown mercy (2:9–10). Their identity arises not from themselves or from the surrounding culture but from the free love of God. Their lives, corporate and individual, are defined by this reality. The consequence of this is that they are social aliens and exiles

(2:11)—a distinct society but not separate unto itself, a community that is recognizably different but not hostile, possessing what has been called "soft difference" (Volf). It is out of this unique identity, as a community called by God, that their new life of righteousness that reflects the character of God receives its form and impetus.

Bibliography

Achtemeier, P. J. *1 Peter*. Hermeneia. Fortress, 1996.

Dryden, J. *Theology and Ethics in 1 Peter: Paraenetic Strategies for Christian Character Formation*. WUNT 2/209. Mohr Siebeck, 2007.

Green, J. B. *1 Peter*. THNTC. Eerdmans, 2007.

Volf, M. "Soft Difference: Theological Reflections on the Relation between Church and Culture in 1 Peter." *ExAud* 10 (1994): 15–30.

◆ 2 Peter ◆

J. de Waal Dryden

Like 1 Peter, this epistle adopts the modes of ancient paraenetic epistles and offers wisdom to a Christian community at a perilous crossroads. The nascent danger is false teachers leading the community away from the apostolic faith. But, perhaps surprisingly, this danger is defined in almost exclusively moral terms. The false teachers are "creatures of instinct" (2:12), who "have eyes full of adultery" and "hearts trained in greed" (2:14). Here, as elsewhere in the NT, heterodoxy and heteropraxis are two sides of the same coin, distinguishable but inseparable. Where one is present, the other is assumed. So while these false teachers are denounced as "ignorant blasphemers" (2:12), the emphasis of the epistle is on the moral threat that they pose, having the ability to "entice unsteady souls" (2:14).

The author's main agenda is not merely to protect the church from false teachers but to lead them in a path of flourishing, where their faith produces recognizable fruits of righteousness and love. This is why the body of the letter begins with its stair-stepping catalog of virtues in 1:5–7: faith, goodness, knowledge, self-control, endurance, godliness, mutual affection, and love. The chief aim of the epistle is the inculcation of these (and other) Christian virtues as a means of and a sign of growth and maturity in Christian character (Charles). The false teachers are an obstacle to this process of sanctification and are denounced as such.

Typical of ancient paraenetic literature, the concern in 2 Peter is with the process of maturation (what the Stoics called *prokopē*), the author using rhetorical techniques that foster the adoption of virtues and the repudiation of vices—for example, the rhetorical strategy of the "two ways," a staple in ancient wisdom literature. In this epistle we have a host of such contrasts. The false teachers, who deceive and corrupt, are contrasted with the apostles, who have given a true witness of Christ that leads to righteousness and glory. The false teachers are associated with archetypal evil characters from the OT, like Balaam, while those who remain faithful to Christ are identified with archetypal characters of faith, like Noah, "a herald of righteousness" (2:5). The false teachers are "waterless springs" (2:17) that lead to destruction, whereas faithfulness to the apostolic witness leads to the "new heaven and the new earth in which righteousness is at home" (3:13). The point of these contrasts is to clarify choices. The author exposes the magnitude of the disparity between them and the apostolic faith in order to force a choice between the two; it is no longer possible to befriend both. In this way, the author safeguards this community from a lethal danger to its progress in the faith.

Bibliography

Bauckham, R. *Jude, 2 Peter*. WBC 50. Word, 1983.

Charles, J. *Virtue amidst Vice: The Catalog of Virtues in 2 Peter 1*. JSNTSup 150. Sheffield Academic Press, 1997.

Green, G. *Jude and 2 Peter*. BECNT. Baker Academic, 2008.

✦ 1–3 John ✦
Ruth Anne Reese

The Johannine Epistles proclaim the person and work of Jesus Christ and the relationship of the reader to him and to the Father. God is both light and love, and God's love is demonstrated through Jesus' sacrifice, which forgives sins (1 John 4:7–11). This sacrifice is the means by which believers live in love, truth, and purity with God and one another. God's love enables those who immerse their lives in God to resist sin and to be like God in character during this life (1 John 3:9). In addition, remaining within the sphere of God's love allows believers to live without fear of death and final judgment (1 John 4:17–18). All three of the epistles emphasize the importance of walking in the truth of one's relationship with Christ (1 John 3:18; 2 John 4; 3 John 4).

These epistles exhort readers to live ethically because of their relationship with God. The foremost aim of believers is to live a life that can be described as "walking with God." In 1 John, this life is made available through the atoning sacrifice of Jesus Christ (2:2), his advocacy for those who sin, including both believers and the whole world (2:2), and by the confession of sin (1:9). The same sacrificial blood that allows believers to walk with God also enables the believer to live in right relationship with others (1:7). It is the believers' relationship with Jesus and through Jesus with the Father that enables them to live in justice, love, truth, and purity (significant themes in the Johannine Epistles). Jesus becomes the source for loving God and loving fellow believers.

Those who want to know if they are living a life that is immersed in God should look to their own actions (1 John 3:14, 18). Love of God is evidenced through obedience rather than solely by verbal affirmation (1 John 2:3). Believers are to obey the "word of God," understood as the command to love God and other believers (1 John 4:21) as well as the instruction to follow the exemplary way of Jesus' sacrifice (1 John 2:6; 3:16). Believers demonstrate their love of God by obeying God's command to love their fellow believers. This is demonstrated in hospitality (2 John 10; 3 John 6) and by the sacrifice of one's life on behalf of others, if needed (1 John 3:16). Conversely, believers demonstrate their true allegiances, with all that is apart from God ("the world"), when they engage in hateful behavior toward others.

Speech is also a significant ethical topic of these epistles. In 1 John a contrast is established between those who make false claims about their relationship with God and the failure to live by the truth, and 2 John is concerned about those who deceive the church (v. 7). The truth of statements is determined by the lifestyle of the speaker (1 John 1:6) and by the assertions that the speaker makes about Jesus (1 John 2:22–23), particularly Jesus' incarnation and his relationship to the Father.

In 1 John there are abundant contrasts between love and hate, light and darkness, truth and lying. In a similar vein, 1 John indicates that those who confess their sins are forgiven and cleansed by God (1:8) and also claims that those who know God do not sin (2:1; 3:6, 9). This apparent contradiction has been the source for significant discussions about whether believers sin. Catholic tradition and many Protestant traditions assert that believers attain perfection either at death or upon entrance into heaven. This understanding attends well to the act of confession on the part of believers but does not easily explain the meaning of 1 John 3:6–9, with its emphasis on the sinless believer. The Wesleyan tradition claims that it is possible for believers to reach perfection in this life by being completely immersed in God's love and glory. This understanding attends well to 1 John 3:6–9 but has to assert that the confession referred to in 1 John 1:8 happens at conversion. The seeming contradiction contrasts the hope that believers will abide in God to such an extent in this life that they will not sin with the reminder that Jesus' sacrifice and advocacy are available for believers also if they have need.

The Johannine Epistles call believers to right relationship with God and others through the work of Jesus. This includes loving others, speaking truth and resisting deceit, imitating Jesus, practicing hospitality, and avoiding all that is counter to God. In the mingling of love, truth, and obedience comes the assurance of relationship with God as God's children.

Bibliography

Smalley, S. *1, 2, 3 John*. WBC 51. Word, 2007.

Wesley, J. "The Great Privilege of Those That Are Born of God." Pages 431–43 in *The Works of John Wesley: Sermons*, ed. A. Outler. Abingdon, 1984.

♦ Jude ♦
J. de Waal Dryden

Jude is a small jewel of pastoral theology, giving guidance to a community in danger of falling out of step with the apostolic faith. This apostasy is described more as an ethical corruption than a doctrinal drift, but both are present. As elsewhere in the NT, "the faith once delivered" refers to more than a synopsis of apostolic teaching; it also incorporates a significant ethical component. Doctrinal corruption and ethical corruption are inseparable twins, always present together.

The source of the corruption is a new group of leaders in the church. These teachers have been accepted as members of the community (v. 12), but Jude is committed to exposing them as immoral corrupters of the community who teach unsound doctrine, plainly seen in the illicit lifestyle that they practice and promote (v. 4). To clarify the danger that these teachers pose to the community, Jude likens them to three reprehensible exemplars from the history of Israel: Cain, Balaam, and Korah (v. 11). In contemporary Jewish apocalyptic literature these three were depicted as deceivers who led Israel astray. Jude intimates that the fate of some in the community will mimic those in Israel who were party to the exodus but died in the desert for their unbelief (v. 5). The pastoral impulse behind this threat of judgment is to clarify the seriousness of the corruption in their midst and to facilitate a return to apostolic beliefs and praxis.

Bibliography

Bauckham, R. *Jude, 2 Peter.* WBC 50. Word, 1983.

Green, G. *Jude and 2 Peter.* BECNT. Baker Academic, 2008.

Reese, R. *2 Peter and Jude.* THNTC. Eerdmans, 2007.

◆ Revelation ◆

Kendra Jo Haloviak

According to D. H. Lawrence, "The Apocalypse of John is, as it stands, the work of a second-rate mind. It appeals intensely to second-rate minds in every country and every century" (12). Apparently, many Christians agree. Finding the book strange and disturbing, most Christian communities rarely read the final book of the Christian canon. Christians who are serious about changing this world find escapist interpretations of Revelation irrelevant. The book is left to fanatics waiting for the world to erupt, while real Christians go about the ministry of Jesus.

Yet, according to the first words of Revelation, Jesus is both the subject and the mediator of the book: "[The] Revelation of Jesus Christ" (1:1). During the mid-1980s Allan Boesak, a Christian preacher and critic of South Africa's apartheid, was allowed one book, the Bible, during months of solitary confinement. Boesak later wrote, "Somehow, I don't know why, I turned to the words of John of Patmos, and for the first time I began to understand. The power of his testimony forever changed my life" (13). For him, the book is precisely for Christians who are serious about the ministry of Jesus to change this world. But how are we to read this work? The present essay discusses the book's genre, the book's social setting, and the use of the book in ethics.

A Liturgical Apocalypse: Revelation's Unique Genre

Although the book of Revelation starts with the Greek word *apokalypsis* ("apocalypse"), its genre is not easy to distinguish. The work refers to itself as a "prophecy" (1:3; 22:7, 10, 18, 19). Yet seven letters are tucked into the first part, and it begins and ends like a first-century epistle (1:4–7; 22:21). Between chapters 4 and 19, sixteen hymns burst through the narrative (Aune 314–17; Harris 4–16). Consequently, most scholars see the book as a hybrid of some sort. For Elisabeth Schüssler Fiorenza, the apocalyptic and liturgical elements serve the book's prophetic goals (164–70). Other scholars emphasize the overarching epistolary format or the characteristics that it shares with other apocalypses.

This generic complexity provides an important key to the interpretation of the book and its ethical implications. If a genre is not merely a mold into which content is poured but rather is inseparable from meaning, then these forms carry various theological perspectives and show the complex nature of the book (Bakhtin; Morson and Emerson 271–305). For example, apocalyptic literature emphasizes a view of God far removed from human experience and in control of the entire cosmos. Typically, the apocalyptic seer must stand far off and watch the mighty actions of God taking place throughout the universe and into the future. In contrast, Christian liturgy embraces a God-with-us who is present in earthly worship experiences. John shows these views of God as they continually collide and collaborate. Using the book to shut down such a "surplus" of theological meaning is fundamentally opposed to the book's very nature (Haloviak 21–108).

Revelation's Social Setting: Ordinary People Resisting Rome

Studies in the book of Revelation still wrestle with many disputed issues, including date of authorship, the author's identity, the work's intended audience(s), and the overall social situations of people living in the province of Asia during the first century CE of the Roman Empire.

Recent studies on provincial imperial cults and life in the major cities of the province of Asia provide a helpful corrective to the assumption, no longer held by most scholars, that Christians underwent harsh persecution during the reign of Domitian (81–96 CE). However, the provincial imperial cult did permeate every aspect of life in the major cities of the Roman provinces (Friesen 23–131). Purchasing food in the marketplace, eating meals in a trade guild banquet, and participating in the regular festivals, games, and intercity competitions all held major implications for one's social status. Although it might be rare for a Christian to be dragged before a Roman provincial leader for refusing to worship at a local shrine, the degree to which a follower of Jesus could participate in city life required daily decisions (Thompson 37). The author of Revelation takes a firm stand against assimilating into Roman culture.

The reality of the provincial imperial cult, along with internal controversies (2:6, 14, 15, 20) and tensions with the local Jewish communities in the cities (2:9; 3:9), posed difficult choices for the first recipients of John's Apocalypse. The book is a call to resist Rome (the "beast" [13:1–18]; the "harlot" [17:1–18]) and all who blur the lines between Rome and the Lamb (like "Jezebel"

[2:18–29]). Members of local congregations who chose to join in the songs of Revelation became witnesses who were willing to lay down their lives rather than compromise with the culture in which they found themselves (11·4–13).

Apocalypse Now and Then: The Book of Revelation's Moral Vision

The Apocalypse, this work of generic (theological) complexity that was originally situated in liturgical experiences calling worshipers to resist the dominant culture, invites readers today to consider its resources for the moral life. The book weaves together worship and ethics. The liturgical moments surround the unfolding drama. After Christians worship, additional action is required: contemporary beasts must be confronted (13:1–18), the collaboration of church and state must be denounced (13:11–17), and the seduction of wealth must be resisted (17:1–18:18). Human lives may not be labeled a commodity to be traded (18:11–13), but rather must be deeply valued in the worshiping community's ongoing commitment to the "healing of the nations" (22:2).

Typically, ethicists considering the use of Scripture in the moral enterprise focus on moral obligations, societal values, or personal virtues. However, the category of moral vision must also be considered. Although last in the NT canon, the book of Revelation should be first in terms of ethical discourse. "Before the message there must be the vision, before the sermon the hymn, before the prose the poem" (Wilder 1). The book of Revelation provides a moral vision that "is a revolution in the imagination. It entails a challenge to view the world in a way that is radically different from the common perception" (Collins 283). The book's future vision—an earth made new (21:1–5)—shapes moral vision, compelling its readers to transform the world.

Bibliography

Aune, D. *Revelation 1–5*. WBC 52A. Word, 1997.

Bakhtin, M. "The Problem of Speech Genres." Pages 60–102 in *Speech Genres and Other Late Essays*, ed. C. Emerson and M. Holquist. University of Texas Press, 1986.

Bauckham, R. *The Theology of the Book of Revelation*. NTT. Cambridge University Press, 1993.

Boesak, A. *Comfort and Protest: The Apocalypse from a South African Perspective*. Westminster, 1987.

Collins, J. *The Apocalyptic Imagination: An Introduction to Jewish Apocalyptic Literature*. 2nd ed. Eerdmans, 1998.

Friesen, S. *Imperial Cults and the Apocalypse of John: Reading Revelation in the Ruins*. Oxford University Press, 2001.

Haloviak, K. "Worlds at War, Nations in Song: Dialogic and Moral Vision in the Hymns of the Book of Revelation." PhD diss., Graduate Theological Union, 2002.

Harris, M. "The Literary Function of Hymns in the Apocalypse of John." PhD diss., Southern Baptist Theological Seminary, 1989.

Lawrence, D. H. *Apocalypse*. Heinemann, 1931.

Morson, G., and C. Emerson. *Mikhail Bakhtin: Creation of a Prosaics*. Stanford University Press, 1990.

Schüssler Fiorenza, E. *The Book of Revelation: Justice and Judgment*. 2nd ed. Fortress, 1998.

Thompson, L. "Ordinary Lives: John and His First Readers." Pages 25–47 in *Reading the Book of Revelation: A Resource for Students*, ed. D. Barr. RBS 44. Society of Biblical Literature, 2003.

Wilder, A. *Theopoetic: Theology and the Religious Imagination*. Fortress, 1976.

5

SELECTED TOPICS
IN NEW TESTAMENT ETHICS

♦ Fruit of the Spirit ♦

Gary M. Simpson

"The fruit of the Spirit" is Paul's metaphor (Gal. 5:22) that he places in contrast to his metaphor "the works of the flesh" (Gal. 5:19). Flesh and Spirit are contrasting powers or "desires" that produce opposing ways of human life together (Gal. 5:17). Paul designates love as the Spirit's first fruit.

Having highlighted this initial contrast of powers, Paul illuminates subsequent contrasts that have ethical import. Second, therefore, "works" in the plural contrasts with "fruit" in the singular. Flesh produces an unhindered plethora of obvious works that divide people from one another and thus hinder people from inheriting God's kingdom. Paul stresses the chaotic plurality of these works, which is comparable to the swamp of evils unleashed on the world when Pandora proverbially opened the box. Spirit, however, produces a singular "fruit" that issues in a flourishing life together led by the Spirit.

Paul's third contrast comes in Gal. 5:18, where life together "led by the Spirit" is distinguished from life together "subject to the law." On the one hand, for Paul, the law has its source in God and thereby is itself always good.

Yet, law always intrinsically embodies a distinctive coercive element in order to gain even a semblance of flourishing human life together. On the other hand, Paul's organic metaphor of fruit stresses the effective yet noncoercive force field of life together in the Spirit. The notion of fruit recalls Jesus' words "every good tree bears good fruit" (Matt. 7:17). Because the Holy Spirit is free and freeing (2 Cor. 3:17; Gal. 5:1), Augustine and those influenced by him stress the spontaneity of the Christian life in the Spirit in contrast to the coercive character of a life together subject to God's law.

With these three contrasts framing Paul's metaphor of fruit of the Spirit, questions often arise about how to think through Paul's lists that follow the powers of flesh and Spirit. It is unlikely that Paul is using any ancient commonplace list of vices or virtues, or that he is giving some kind of specifically Christian comprehensive listing of vices or virtues. Some interpreters have thought that Paul is referencing three groups of three virtues, but others have rightly found that idea not persuasive or fruitful for ethical reflection. That Paul says "and things like these" and "such things" (Gal. 5:21, 23) indicates the illustrative and thereby nonexhaustive nature of these listings.

One significant suggestion made first by Augustine and taken up again by Martin Luther, among others, is that Paul places love as the first fruit of the Spirit because love is really the only virtue of Christian life together. In this view, love issues from faith in Christ, which is created by the Spirit (Rom. 5:5; 1 Cor. 13; Gal. 5:6). Christ becomes the one form of Christian faith and freedom—"Love one another as I have loved you" (John 15:12) (see Bonhoeffer). Indeed, this "as I have loved you" "expands into all" (Luther 93) aspects of the Christian life together producing, forming, and norming whatever other subsequent virtues are needed in order to serve neighbors and their neighborhoods and communities. Whether the neighbor is within or without the Christian church appears unimportant (Rom. 13:8–10; Gal. 5:13–14). Love seeking justice operates like a pluripotent stem cell becoming through Christian discernment whatever set of virtues neighbors, neighborhoods, and communities need for their welfare, thus setting out the breadth of Christian vocation in God's world.

The Augustinian-Lutheran trajectory opens a more discernment-oriented model of Christian ethical reflection that focuses on the necessities and needs of neighbors and their neighborhoods and communities. This contrasts with the "third use of the law" model of Christian ethical reflection, initiated by Philip Melanchthon and John Calvin, which focuses Christian ethical reflection more on identifying, following, and applying the particulars of biblical injunctions and commands. On the one hand, the "fruit of the Spirit" approach to ethical reflection based on discerning love seeking justice for the neighbor resonates with the centrality of prudence within classical and medieval natural law approaches to ethics, still championed by many contemporary Roman Catholic moral theologians. On the other hand, the "third use of the law" approach, which looks to biblical laws and NT injunctions as superior rules that guide Christian life, has largely rejected Christian natural-law reasoning.

Bibliography

Bonhoeffer, D. "Ethics as Formation." Pages 76–102 in *Ethics*. Fortress, 2005.

Boyce, J. "The Poetry of the Spirit." *WW* 20 (2000): 290–98.

Grabill, S. *Rediscovering the Natural Law in Reformed Theological Ethics*. Eerdmans, 2006.

Longenecker, R. *Galatians*. WBC 41. Word, 1990.

Luther, M. *Lectures on Galatians, 1535*. Ed. J. Pelikan. 2 vols. Concordia, 1963–64.

Martyn, J. *Galatians*. AB 33A. Doubleday, 1997.

Plumer, E. *Augustine's Commentary on Galatians*. OECS. Oxford University Press, 2003.

Porter, J. *Nature as Reason: A Thomistic Theory of Natural Law*. Eerdmans, 2005.

◆ Golden Rule ◆

Michael Westmoreland-White

The Golden Rule is the designation for Jesus' command to his disciples in the Sermon on the Mount: "[Therefore] in everything do to others as you would have them do to you; for this is the law and the prophets" (Matt. 7:12; cf. Luke 6:31).

Mark 12:31 and Rom. 13:9 similarly indicate that the law is summed up by the command "You shall love your neighbor as yourself," a quotation from Lev. 19:18. This suggests that Jesus' formulation likewise refers to Lev. 19:18.

The appearance of "therefore" in Matt. 7:12 indicates that the Golden Rule is based on God's trustworthiness and mercy in Matt. 7:11. Similarly, Mark 12:31; Luke 6:31–36; and Lev. 19:18 link the Golden Rule with God's gracious mercy as the Lord. God does not merely reciprocate; God initiates.

Versions of this principle are found in many world religions. For example, in Hinduism there is the saying "This is the sum of duty: do not do to others what would cause pain for you" (*Mahababharata* 5.1517); in Confucianism, "Do not do to others what you would not have them do for you" (*Analects of*

Confucius 15:23); in Buddhist writings, "Hurt not others in ways you yourself would find hurtful" (*Udana-Varga* 5.18); in ancient Greek philosophy, "May I do to others as I would they should do unto me" (Plato, *Laws* II); in Judaism, in addition to Lev. 19:18, "Do not do to your neighbor what is hateful to you; this is the whole Law, all else is commentary" (*b. Šabb.* 31a), and "What you hate, do not do to anyone" (Tob. 4:15).

The Golden Rule thus functions, both in Jesus' teaching and elsewhere, as an overarching principle of initiating what one wishes others to reciprocate. It seeks to form in persons an other-centered view of the universe. Parents and teachers have used it to help form virtues of caring and hospitality. The early church received this precept in both negative and positive formulations (Luz 427).

The parallels in many different moral systems suggest to many that this precept fits the created order and is evidence of "general revelation" (apart from the special revelation in Scripture) or "natural law." Removed from the context of the rest of Jesus' teaching on God's mercy and trustworthiness as guiding norm, the Golden Rule is neither unique nor the most radical of Jesus' teachings. It and other religious moral standards stand in stark contrast to the laissez-faire ethic of the marketplace that makes self-interest the guiding virtue.

Bibliography

Bauman, C. *The Sermon on the Mount: The Modern Quest for Its Meaning.* Mercer University Press, 1985.

Luz, U. *Matthew 1–7.* Trans. W. Linss. CC. Fortress, 1992.

Schrage, W. *The Ethics of the New Testament.* Trans. D. Green. Fortress, 1987.

Stassen, G. *Living the Sermon on the Mount: Practical Hope for Grace and Deliverance.* Jossey-Bass, 2006.

Verhey, A. *The Great Reversal: Ethics and the New Testament.* Eerdmans, 1984.

♦ Healthcare Systems in Scripture ♦

Joel B. Green

"Healthcare system" refers to the network of beliefs, resources, institutions, and strategies in the maintenance of health and the identification and treatment of sickness. Integral to a healthcare system are assumptions about the etiology and diagnosis of sickness, judgments concerning acceptable and unacceptable options for therapeutic intervention in cases of sickness, and a person's capacity to access healthcare options.

Scripture refers to the restoration of health by a number of options, including the body's capacity to self-heal, prayer and other forms of divine entreaty, and such therapeutic interventions as the intercession of a gifted healer, care within the household, use of traditional medicaments, or employment of a professional physician. The Bible explicitly rejects recourse to magic and generally views physicians with disdain. This is largely because, within Scripture, healing practices are guided by the recognition that Yahweh alone is the source of life and, therefore, the source of renewed health.

Perspectives on Sickness and Healing

Medical anthropologists understand that different societies construct in varying ways how their members think about and respond to sickness and healing. One society identifies a certain condition within the boundaries of its definition of health, while another views that same condition as sickness. Moreover, different societies provide different accounts of sickness, with each both identifying the etiology or cause of the sickness and indicating the therapeutic interventions necessary for recovery of health. One widely used classification of sickness introduces three categories (Hahn).

First, "disease accounts" focus on the body of the individual as the source of sickness. Patients are treated as individuals, with the site of disease sought in the structure and function of bodily organs and functions. Biomedical interventions serve as the primary mode of therapy.

Second, "illness accounts" identify patients as embodied persons in a nest of relationships. The cause and treatment of sicknesses thus require attention to persons in their social environments, with recovery of health measured not only in biomedical but also in relational terms.

Third, "disorder accounts" focus not only on the patient's body and social networks but also on the cosmic order of things. "When the universe is unbalanced, sickness may be manifested in particular locales and individual patients" (Hahn 28).

Of course, this is a catalog of ideal types, with actual accounts of sickness and recovery blurring the lines between these categories. The importance of such a classification rests in our recognition that, for most of our contemporaries in the modern West, sickness is understood in terms of disease accounts—indeed, our healthcare systems are dominated by biomedical diagnoses and therapies—whereas related legislation or narrated episodes of sickness and healing in the biblical materials are typically illness or disorder accounts.

As an example, consider the case of "leprosy," which in the Bible is rarely if ever true leprosy (Hansen's disease), but instead includes any of a number of skin conditions. Leviticus 13–14 commands that persons diagnosed by a priest (acting as a kind of healthcare consultant) as lepers be quarantined. In this case, "leprosy" is not life threatening from a biomedical point of view, nor is this skin disease contagious. Instead, the contagion is ritual impurity. "Leprosy" thus exemplifies how religious, social, and physical considerations coalesce in a single diagnosis. Cases of exorcism similarly correlate what might appear to moderns as discrete spiritual, social, mental, and physical factors, both in the presentation of the disorder and in its resolution (see, e.g., Luke 8:26–39).

The integration of measures of human well-being is crucial to a world in which healing and sickness are indicators of Yahweh's favor and displeasure. Although one cannot argue that health is necessarily the direct result of God's favor or that sickness is necessarily the direct result of divine punishment, it is true that for ancient Israel there could be a causal link from sin to sickness (see, e.g., Deut. 28; 1 Kgs. 13:1–25; Prov. 3:28–35; 11:19; 13:13–23; 1 Cor. 11:29–30).

Healthcare Practices

Healthcare practices in Israel centered in the home, where the sick were kept, and where care might take the form of maintaining vigil and soliciting the help of Yahweh through prayer and fasting (e.g., 2 Sam. 12:15–23). Women in childbirth received the aid of midwives (e.g., Gen. 35:17; 38:28). Only rarely do physicians appear in the OT. When they do, they are typically seen as negative alternatives to Yahweh (e.g., 2 Chr. 16:12; Jer. 8:22–9:6) or as persons offering worthless advice (Job 13:4). In the OT, faithfulness to Yahweh explicitly excluded magic (or sorcery, the manipulation of the spirits) as a remedy, in preference to divine intervention and care (e.g., Lev. 19:26–28; Deut. 18:10–14; Ezek. 13:17–18). This is consistent with the biblical portrait of Yahweh as the God to whom Israel must be exclusively loyal. It is also consistent with the state of medical knowledge in antiquity and thus with the mysteriousness of the human body and its processes, which encouraged hope in magic and/or miracle.

Physicians. Prejudice against physicians is not unique to the OT world. For example, Cato's advice to his son to stay clear of doctors, preferring instead "a little book of prescriptions for curing those who were sick in his family" (Plutarch, *Cato Maj.* 23.3–6), reflects a Roman preference for traditional healing practices over Greek medicine as well as Cato's rejection of fee-based, professional medicine. In rural areas of the Roman Empire, snake charmers and healers with magical powers were the norm. In pandemic times, however, all eyes turned toward the gods for defense and salvation.

Physicians were sufficiently common in the NT world that Jesus could allude to their activity metaphorically (e.g., Mark 2:17 pars.). Only the wealthy could afford the care of a trained physician, however, and village people were especially vulnerable to the abuse of charlatans. Mark 5:26 is illustrative: "She had endured much under many physicians, and had spent all that she had; and she was no better, but rather grew worse." Not surprisingly, then, Jesus' followers were advised against charging for their healthcare interventions: "Cure the sick, raise the dead, cleanse the lepers, cast out demons. You received without payment; give without payment" (Matt. 10:8 [cf. *Did.* 11]).

Village and rural folk depended less on persons who publicly professed the physician's oath, and they found the prospect of divine healing especially attractive (e.g., Acts 5:16). Hospitality might take the form of healthcare (e.g., Luke 10:30–35; Acts 16:33–34), and the author of 1 Timothy reflects medical tradition when he advises "a little wine for the sake of your stomach and your frequent ailments" (5:23 [for a registry of practical medicaments, see Pliny the Elder, *Nat.* 23–32]). Relative wealth could not certify medical competence, however. Medical treatises might sneer at root cutters, drug sellers, and purveyors of amulets and incantations, but even the best physicians understood little of the ways of the body.

Agents of healing. Throughout the OT, Yahweh's role as healer is paramount: "I am the LORD who heals you" (Exod. 15:26 [see also, e.g., 2 Kgs. 5:7; Isa. 57:19]). The prophet Ezekiel portrays Yahweh as healer of the weak, the sick, and the lost (Ezek. 34:16). Yahweh binds up and heals the wounded (Job 5:17–18).

In the NT, the role of God as healer is continued, but now healing is a sign of the inbreaking kingdom of God. According to the book of Acts, God worked deeds of power through Jesus so as to accredit him as God's authorized agent of salvation (2:22); likewise, the Lord "testified to the word of his grace by granting signs and wonders to be done" through Paul and Barnabas (14:3). Others may participate in God's healing activity, but this does not detract from the identification of Yahweh as the source of healing.

In the OT, prophets sometimes were portrayed as agents of healing. Elijah was instrumental in restoring a widow's son to life (1 Kgs. 17:8–24), and Elisha instructed Naaman, commander of the Syrian army, how to be cured of leprosy (2 Kgs. 5:1–15). According to the Synoptic Gospels, Jesus' disciples participated in his ministries of healing and exorcism (Mark 6:7–13 pars.), and in Acts, the apostles and other witnesses healed in the name of Jesus (e.g., 3:1–10; 9:34; 16:16–18). In 1 Cor. 12, Paul lists the gifts of healing and working of miracles as manifestations of the work of the Spirit in the life of the church. In his letter, James directs those who are sick to call for the elders of the church to pray over them, anointing them with oil in the name of the Lord (5:15–16). Correlating confession and healing, James emphasizes healing as integral to the integrity of the Christian community.

Bibliography

Albl, M. "'Are Any among You Sick?' The Health Care System in the Letter of James." *JBL* 121 (2002): 123–43.

Avalos, H. *Health Care and the Rise of Christianity*. Hendrickson, 1999.

Hahn, R. *Sickness and Healing: An Anthropological Perspective*. Yale University Press, 1995.

◆ Kingdom of God ◆
Bruce Chilton

In all of Jesus' teaching no idea is more important, more central, or more resonant than the kingdom of God. The kingdom of God is also a vital concept in the Scriptures of Israel (which Christians call the Old Testament). By referring to the kingdom, both Jesus and prophets before him focused on God as the king of the universe, the fundamental force behind all that is, and on God's role in shaping human experience. Jesus embraced this prophetic principle and gave it his own unique meaning.

The promise of the kingdom is that people will finally come to realize divine justice and peace in all that they do. People will put into action with one another the righteousness they see in God. So the kingdom is a matter of vision, of perceiving God at work both in the present and in the future, but it is also a matter of ethics. Jesus made the kingdom of God the center of his preaching as well as of his activity, and it remains the pivot of Christian theology.

Whether in present experience or in hope for the future, the kingdom of God was celebrated in ancient Israel in five ways, all closely related. The book of Psalms clearly reflects this celebration of the kingdom, and Jesus also taught that the kingdom could be known in these ways. Because the kingdom is a power within human beings, and not an entity alien to them, to understand it requires more than a simple definition. Instead, both the psalms and Jesus referred to the kingdom according to how its force could be perceived and how that force would shape all human life.

First, the kingdom of God is behind the whole of created life, the creativity that makes life possible, but at the same time it is beyond the immediate comprehension of any living thing. For that reason, the psalms portray the kingdom as so near as to seem present in time and tangible and yet ultimate and distant from the point of view of what its full disclosure will be like:

> Say among the nations, "The LORD is king!
> The world is firmly established;
>   it shall never be moved.
> He will judge the peoples with equity." (Ps. 96:10)

All peoples are finally to know, when God judges, the truth that is even now celebrated and sung by some people. Those who sing, the group that joins in order to recite this psalm, recognize now, not just in the future, that "the world is firmly established; it shall never be moved." The wonderful order of the universe invites the psalmic community to rejoice in God's power in the present and to anticipate his full revelation in the future.

Second, just as the kingdom cannot be contained by time, it being a reality both in the present and the future, so also it is transcendent in space. The usual setting of Israel's praise is in the temple, where the psalms typically were sung, but every part of the creation will come to acknowledge what is known there:

> All your works shall give thanks to you, O LORD,
>   and all your faithful shall bless you.
> They shall speak of the glory of your kingdom,
>   and tell of your power,
> to make known to all people your mighty deeds,
>   and the glorious splendor of your kingdom.
> Your kingdom is an everlasting kingdom,
>   and your dominion endures throughout all generations. (Ps.
>   145:10, 13)

All creatures are to give thanks to the Lord, but it is his faithful in particular who are said to bless him. What is rehearsed in the temple, the "might of the awesome deeds" of God, is to be acknowledged by humanity as a whole (Ps. 145:6).

Third, the kingdom is an insistent force of justice that will ultimately prevail. The kingdom is ever righteous, but it attains to a consummation:

> Break the arm of the wicked and evildoers;
>   seek out their wickedness until you find none.

> The LORD is king forever and ever;
>   the nations shall perish from his land. (Ps. 10:15–16)

The punishment of the wicked is the dark side of the blessing of the poor; the vindication of the meek, the fatherless, and the oppressed (Ps. 10:17–18) requires a reversal in the fortunes of those who do evil in order to be realized.

Fourth, human entry into the kingdom depends on what people do. Psalm 24 poses and answers a question that is central to the religion of Israel as reflected in the biblical tradition:

> Who shall ascend the hill of the LORD?
> And who shall stand in his holy place?
> Those who have clean hands and pure hearts,
>   who do not lift up their souls to what is false,
>   and do not swear deceitfully. (vv. 3–4)

The point is that purity is effected by one's ethical behavior as well as by the practices of purification (such as bathing and abstention from sexual intercourse) that conventionally were requisites for ascending the mount of the temple.

Fifth, Ps. 47 evokes how the recognition of God is to radiate from Zion when it identifies "the people of the God of Abraham" as "the princes of the peoples":

> The princes of the peoples gather as the people of the God of
>   Abraham.
> For the shields of the earth belong to God;
>   he is highly exalted. (v. 9)

Israel is the nucleus of the larger group of those who recognize the God of Abraham. From its center, the power of the kingdom is to radiate outward to include within its recognition peoples beyond the usual range of Israel.

Jesus articulated all five of these ways of seeing God's kingdom because he understood that they conveyed the mystery of the kingdom. He taught his disciples to pray to God, "Your kingdom come" (Matt. 6:10; Luke 11:2), because he hoped for it to be fully present to all people. In Aramaic, he really said that the kingdom "will" come; he was not merely wishing for it to come. In the same way that God's presence can be sensed now, he taught, his followers should also welcome its coming in the future.

Jesus' belief that the kingdom is transcendent, capable of displacing other powers, comes through clearly in one of his most famous sayings: "If it is by the spirit of God that I cast out demons, then the kingdom of God has come to you" (Matt. 12:28; cf. Luke 11:20). For Jesus, exorcism was not an esoteric or magical practice but a matter of confronting evil with the power of divine justice. He typically called demons "unclean spirits." For Jesus, people taken on their own were as clean as God had made Adam and Eve. If a person became unclean or impure, it was not because of contact with exterior objects. Instead, impurity was a disturbance in one's own spirit, the "unclean spirit" that made a person want to be impure. To his mind, uncleanness arrived not from material contagion but rather from the disturbed desire that people conceive to pollute and do harm to themselves. Uncleanness had to be dealt with in the inward, spiritual personality of those afflicted. Jesus believed that God's Spirit was a far more vital force than the unclean spirits that disturbed humanity. Against demonic infection a greater, countercontagion could prevail, the positive energy of God's purity.

Entry into the kingdom is also the dominant image in Jesus' famous statement about wealth: "It is easier for a camel to go through the eye of a needle than for someone who is rich to enter the kingdom of God" (Mark 10:25; cf. Matt. 19:24; Luke 18:25). This dedication to justice, the third dimension of the kingdom, leads on naturally to the fourth: Jesus needed to cope with the issue of defilement as one member of Israel (with a certain set of practices) met with another member of Israel (with another set of practices). To deal with that question, a single aphorism of Jesus was precisely designed: "There is nothing outside a person that by going in can defile, but the things that come out are what defile" (Mark 7:15). Finally, in the course of Jesus' occupation of the temple, Mark has Jesus articulate the dimension of the kingdom's radiance: "Is it not written, 'My house shall be called a house of prayer for all the nations'? But you have made it a den of robbers" (Mark 11:17).

In Jesus' teaching, the five coordinates of the kingdom become the dynamics of the kingdom, the ways in which God is active with his people. Because God as kingdom is active, response to him is active, not only cognitive. The kingdom of God is a matter of performing the hopeful dynamics of God's revelation to his people. For that reason, Jesus' teaching was not merely a matter of making statements, however carefully crafted and remembered. He also engaged in characteristic activities, a conscious performance of the kingdom, which invited Israel to enter into the reality that he also portrayed in words. Once experience and activity are taken to be the terms of reference of the kingdom, what one does is also an instrument of its revelation, an aspect of its radiance. Jesus' awareness of that caused him to act as programmatically as he spoke, to make of his total activity a parable of the kingdom.

One of the most profound challenges of Jesus' teaching as a whole is that the kingdom of God is not merely for him to perform, but also for all who perceive it. Both the perception of the kingdom and the imperative to act on one's perception are developed by a type of speech well known within Judaism at the time of Jesus: the parable. The Hebrew term rendered by Greek *parabolē* and English "parable" is *māšāl*, which basically refers to a comparison. For that reason, the genre as a whole is an exploration of metaphorical possibilities, as is evidenced, for example, in the book of Proverbs (which in Hebrew is called *mišlê*, illustrating that the term *māšāl* has a wider sense than any single term in English conveys).

The book of Ezekiel represents the wide range of meaning involved. In the name of the Lord, the prophet says, "There is nothing for you in parabling [*mōšlîm*] this parable [*māšāl*]: 'The fathers ate sour grapes, and the children's teeth stand on edge'" (Ezek. 18:2 [translation mine]). Evidently, there is no requirement of a strong narrative element within the metaphorical image for the "parable" to stand as such. Its gist is transparent, and that is precisely what the prophet is objecting to and refuting. Yet within the same book a parable is developed in such an elaborate way that it may be styled an allegory (complete with explanation) in which the fate of Israel between Babylon and Egypt is addressed by comparison to two eagles and a sprig of cedar (Ezek. 17). It is fortunate the chapter includes interpretation because this particular parable (translated as "allegory" at 17:2 in the NRSV) is complicated, opaque, and unrealistic. Nathan's parable of the ewe lamb in 2 Sam. 12:1–15 is a more successful development of narrative allegory and interpretation, and it is not in the least surprising that David got the point of the parable, because a certain didacticism is evident here (as in the narrative parable in Ezek. 17).

Jesus was known as a master of the parable genre in its full extent, from simple adage to complicated, sometimes even surreal, narrative. For that reason, it is only to be expected that the parabolic tradition will have been the outcome of considerable embellishment during the course of transmission. The interest here is not in attribution but in the depth and range of the development of the genre.

Taxed with the charge that his exorcisms were performed by the power of Satan, Jesus replied with the observation that no kingdom or home divided against itself can stand (Matt. 12:24–25; Mark 3:22–25; Luke 11:15–17). That double maxim is devastating enough to have lived on within proverbial tradition of many languages (with a meaning usually unrelated to its original context), but the Gospels also add a parable with a narrative element: the comparison with attempting to rob a strong man's house (Matt. 12:29; Mark 3:27; developed more fully in Luke 11:21–22). Such examples instance not only the range of the genre but also the ease with which one sort of parable might be associated with another. (For that reason, unlike some recent treatments, no hard-and-fast distinction is suggested here between simple, embellished, and narrative parables; a single *māšāl* can easily participate in several features of the genre overall.) The narrative element that was perennially an option within the genre is exploited, complete with an interpretation of the allegory in the parable of the sower (Matt. 13:3–8, 18–23; Mark 4:3–8, 13–20; Luke 8:5–8, 11–15). Although no less didactic than the parable in Ezek. 17, here a certain vivid mastery is instanced.

Rabbinic parables offer analogies to those of Jesus. In a parable of Johanan ben Zakkai (*b. Šabb.* 153a), a king invited his servants to a feast without announcing the hour of the meal. Wise servants attired themselves properly and waited at the door of the king's palace. Foolish servants expected definite signs of the meal's preparation and went about their work until they should see them. When the king suddenly summoned the servants, the wise servants enjoyed a fine meal, while the foolish, work-soiled servants were made to stand and watch.

The motif of a festal banquet is central within Jesus' parables and sayings, and the Matthean parable of the wedding feast (Matt. 22:1–14; cf. Luke 14:16–24) especially invites comparison with that of ben Zakkai. Matthew's subplot concerning the appropriate wedding garment (22:11–13) provides another point of similarity. Still, the meanings generated by the two parables are distinctive. Where ben Zakkai speaks of servants who either are or are not prudent in their assessment of the king's capacity, Jesus speaks of guests invited to a feast who respond with extraordinarily bad and finally violent behavior that is answered in kind. Beneath that distinction, of course, there is a thematic similarity. The readiness to accept and act upon the invitation is called for, especially since the king is none other than God. But each parable urges a particular kind of response upon the hearer. Ben Zakkai's narrative involves dropping normal obligations to await God's promised banquet, while Jesus' parable of recalcitrant guests is more fraught in its warning against obstinacy.

Perhaps most important, comparison with rabbinic parables reveals what often has been overlooked: surrealism is possible within the genre, from Ezekiel through Jesus and on to ben Zakkai. Parables are not just lively stories taken from nature; the point often can turn on what is striking, peculiar, or unpredictable. Even in Jesus' parables of growth, elements of hyperbole are plain. In the narrative of the man, the seed, and the earth (Mark 4:26–29), action is abrupt and unmotivated. The man sleeps for no apparent reason, and he puts in his sickle "immediately"; the seed sprouts in no stated time, and the earth produces "as of itself." Similarly, a mustard seed becomes a "tree" (Matt. 13:31–32; Luke 13:18–19) or makes "big branches" (Mark 4:30–32) without an interval of time being indicated. The point lies in the contrast between beginning and result, miraculous transformation rather than predictable process.

The hyperbolic comparison of start and finish is evident also in the parable of the leaven (Matt. 13:33; Luke 13:20–21). The parables of the hidden treasure and of the pearl (Matt. 13:44–46) are surprising rather than hyperbolic when they concern the discovery of what is valuable, but the reaction of those who find them, in selling everything to acquire them, is exaggerated. In these cases, also, ethical themes are especially conveyed by the least realistic motifs.

Like the prophets, Jesus taught his hearers how to see as well as how to act on the basis of what they saw. Vision—the capacity to perceive God actively at work—is the prophetic foundation of calling people to work with God. In the Judaism of Jesus' time it was said that every Israelite, every day, took up "the yoke of the kingdom of heaven" (*m. Ber.* 2.2). The underlying image puts Israelites in the role of beasts of burden, yoked in harness in order to discharge the duties for which they were intended. Then, if they do in fact accept obedience, they prove themselves innocent of the accusation leveled at them by Isaiah: "The ox knows its owner, and the donkey its master's crib; but Israel does not know, my people do not understand" (Isa.1:3).

The moment of yoking oneself to God's kingdom was at the time of reciting one of the principal texts of Judaism, the Shema:

> Hear, O Israel: the LORD our God, the LORD alone. You shall love the LORD your God with all your heart, and with all your soul, and with all your might. Keep these words that I am commanding you today in your heart. Recite them to your children and talk about them when you are at home and when you are away, when you lie down and when you rise. (Deut. 6:4–7)

When asked about the "first commandment" in the Torah, of course, Jesus cited this one (Mark 12:29–30). In addition, in a famous saying he urged his followers to learn from him, "because my yoke is easy, and my burden is light" (Matt. 11:30). The motif of the "easy" (or "good" [Gk. *chrēstos*]) yoke is a shared metaphor that links Jesus with the rabbinic language that emerged in documents from the second century and later.

But in this case as in others, the sharing of language, when viewed contextually, reveals vital differences. The rabbinic "yoke" connects the Israelite to the Torah; Jesus' "yoke" links the disciple to God's kingdom. Profound lines of cleavage, and of controversy, emanate from that distinction. In Jesus' conception, this divine presence was the force behind the kingdom of God. As he said to Peter, James, and John just before his transfiguration, "There are some standing here who will not taste death until they see that the kingdom of God has come with power" (Mark 9:1 [cf. Matt. 16:28; Luke 9:27]). In the Jewish tradition of this time, both Moses and Elijah were thought to have been immortal; like

Elijah taken up in God's chariot, Moses too was believed to have gone alive into heaven. This saying of Jesus about those who lived in God's presence, people such as Moses and Elijah (but also, in Jesus' view, Abraham, Isaac, and Jacob), showed the way for humanity as a whole. "The kingdom of God has come with power" expresses in a single phrase how Jesus anticipated that God would definitively transform the world as human beings can know the world.

Genuine transformation is a frightening prospect. It involves altering all the usual points of reference that people use to know who they are, where they are, and what they can do to improve their lives. "The kingdom of God has come with power" refers to a complete alteration of conventional reality. The phrase resonates with works that depict the apocalyptic dissolution of both social institutions and the tangible, physical world. The final chapter of the book of Zechariah, for example, predicted that Israel would envelop all the nations in an ultimate sacrifice on Mount Zion in the midst of warfare, destruction, earthquake, and plague. The Aramaic version of the book sets out that apocalypse in language like Jesus':

> And the kingdom of the LORD shall be revealed upon all the inhabitants of the earth; at that time they shall serve before the LORD with one accord, for his name is established in the world; there is none apart from him. (Targum Zechariah 14.9 [departures from the Hebrew text in italics])

To Jesus, this expectation was not merely a matter of symbolism or an expectation that could be passively awaited. Instead, he acted upon the apocalyptic scenario of transformation in order to actively join God in establishing his kingdom. His last public action—his intervention in the normal operation of the temple in Jerusalem—enacted the prophecy of Zechariah, particularly in its Aramaic version: "And there shall never again be a trader in the sanctuary of the Lord of hosts at that time" (Targum Zechariah 14.21b).

Putting those words into practice also put Jesus into direct opposition to Caiaphas, the high priest who had authorized the selling and buying inside the temple to which Jesus objected violently. He intervened with force and threw out both the vendors and their animals (Matt. 21:12–17; Mark 11:11–18; Luke 19:45–48; John 2:13–20).

This act is the key to why Jesus was crucified by the Romans, who had put their prestige behind the status quo in the temple. Although almost every claim ever asserted about Jesus has been subject to dispute, the fact of this forceful intervention is a matter of historical fact. More important than the details of Jesus' action for an understanding of the prophetic force he wished to unleash, however, is the total vision of which Zechariah's prophecy of the cleansing of the temple of commerce is a part. Jesus assimilated Zechariah's vision into his own and made it a programmatic part of his action.

Three key texts in Zechariah set out characteristic concerns of Jesus' message:

> Thus says the Lord of hosts: I will save my people from the east country and from the west country; and I will bring them to live in Jerusalem. They shall be my people and I will be their God, in faithfulness and in righteousness. (8:7–8)

> These are the things that you shall do: Speak the truth to one another, render in your gates judgments that are true and make for peace, do not devise evil in your hearts against one another, and love no false oath; for all these are things that I hate, says the Lord. (8:16–17)

> Thus says the Lord of hosts: The fast of the fourth month, and the fast of the fifth, and the fast of the seventh, and the fast of the tenth, shall be seasons of joy and gladness, and cheerful festivals for the house of Judah: therefore love truth and peace. (8:19)

Very often an ancient misunderstanding arises in the minds of modern readers of the Bible. A false contrast portrays "the God of the Old Testament" as violent and vengeful, while Jesus preached "the God of mercy." But Jesus also was willing to resort to violence, and these prophecies of Zechariah, themselves in line with other prophetic messages in the OT, show that Jesus was directly inspired by the prophets.

When Jesus said, "Many will come from east and west and will eat with Abraham and Isaac and Jacob in the kingdom of heaven" (Matt. 8:11 [cf. Luke 13:29]), he echoed Zechariah (8:7–8). When he spoke of love of God and love of neighbor as summing up the Torah (Matt. 22:34–40; Mark 12:28–34; Luke 10:25–28), he developed a principle that Zechariah had stated (8:16–17). When he offended many of his contemporaries in Judaism by insisting that feasting, not fasting, was to be the rule in the kingdom of God (Matt. 9:14–17; Mark 2:18–22; Luke 5:33–39), he was announcing the new prophetic era (Zech. 8:19) of rejoicing.

By better understanding where Jesus' teaching came from, how it derived from the prophetic tradition that fed his vision and encouraged his demand for justice and ethical action, we can also better see where it was intended to lead his followers. With the prophets before him, Jesus not only insisted on righteousness from individuals but also wanted communities to live by just judgment. Zechariah summarized centuries of the prophetic imperatives when he said, "Thus says the LORD of hosts: Render true judgments, show kindness and mercy to one another; do not oppress the widow, the orphan, the alien, or the poor; and do not devise evil in your hearts against one another" (7:9–10).

In Zechariah's prophecy, as in Jesus' Sermon on the Mount, there is no such thing as requirements for individuals that are separate from human behavior in community. How could there be, when love is at the foundation of the prophetic ethic? That is why, in Zechariah's imperative, God moves from what the community must do ("render true judgments") to what individual Israelites must accomplish ("show kindness and mercy to one another"). Both parts of this single imperative to righteousness appear in the plural: Zechariah, like Moses before him and Jesus after him, is addressing his message to people in their totality, living in community and also conscious of themselves as individuals.

Bibliography

Chilton, B. *Pure Kingdom: Jesus' Vision of God*. SHJ. Eerdmans, 1996.

Grappe, C. *Le Royaume de Dieu: Avant, avec et après Jésus*. MdB 42. Labor et Fides, 2001.

Jeremias, J. *Das Königtum Gottes in den Psalmen: Israels Begegnung mit dem kanaän-aischen Mythos in den Jahwe-König-Psalmen*. FRLANT 141. Vandenhoeck & Ruprecht, 1987.

———. *The Parables of Jesus*. SCM, 1963.

McKnight, S. *A New Vision for Israel: The Teachings of Jesus in National Context*. SHJ. Eerdmans, 1999.

Weiss, J. *Jesus' Proclamation of the Kingdom of God*. Fortress, 1971.

♦ Lists of Vices and Virtues ♦

David J. Downs

Vice and virtue lists refer to the ancient literary form, adapted by biblical writers, in which authors group together dispositions and/or actions to be avoided or embraced. Thus, when the apostle Paul describes the "fruit of the Spirit" as "love, joy, peace, patience, kindness, generosity, faithfulness, gentleness, and self-control" (Gal. 5:22–23), this catalog of virtues fits broadly within an established literary form in the Greco-Roman world.

Context

To the extent that any religion or philosophical system focuses on the cultivation of praiseworthy deeds and the avoidance of immoral actions, inventories of acceptable and unacceptable behavior are customary. Antecedents for and parallels to the biblical vice and virtue lists are found in numerous ancient sources. In the Greco-Roman world in particular, a rich tradition of philosophical reflection on the nature and demonstration of virtue (*aretē*) is the context for the development of the distinct literary form of the virtue and/or vice list. Plato's famous classification of the four cardinal virtues (*aretai*) as wisdom (*phronēsis*), temperance (*sōphrosynē*), justice (*dikaiosynē*), and courage (*andreia*) set the stage for a converse listing of four vices in Hellenistic philosophical writings, particularly in the Stoic tradition (e.g., Plato, *Resp.* 4.427–445). These cardinal vices are typically identified as folly (*aphrosynē*), licentiousness (*akolasia*), injustice (*adikia*), and cowardice (*deilia*), although the fourfold scheme of virtues and vices frequently is divided and expanded. Lists of virtues and vices can run into the dozens and even hundreds (see Aristotle, *Virtues and Vices*; Cicero, *Tusc.* 4.11–38; Diogenes Laertius, *Lives* 7.54). In the Hellenistic world, therefore, virtue and vice catalogs emerged as a literary form that played an important role in moral exhortation and instruction.

Numerous writings from ancient Israel emphasize sin and obedience, yet no precise examples of the fixed literary form of Hellenistic virtue and vice lists are found in the OT. Prophetic denunciations of Judah and Israel's disobedience in Jer. 7:9 and Hos. 4:1–2 do itemize transgressions against the Decalogue (cf. Prov. 6:16–19; 8:13), but these are catalogs of sinful behavior against the Decalogue and not reflections on virtue and vice as character traits. In Jewish literature of the Second Temple period, however, catalogs of virtue and vice become increasingly common, reflecting the influence of Hellenistic thought and literary patterns on Jewish authors (see, e.g., Wis. 8:7; 14:22–27; 4 Macc. 1:2–4; 5:23–24; *T. Reu.* 3.3–8; *T. Levi.* 17.11; Philo, *Sacrifices* 20–33; *Alleg. Interp.* 1.86–87). Related to the virtue and vice lists, though not identical to the literary form, is the "two ways" motif that emphasized the sharp division between the way of life and the way of death (see Deut. 30:19; Prov. 2:12–15; Jer. 21:8; Sir. 21:10; 1QS 3.13–4.26; *Did.* 1–6; *Barn.* 18–21).

Biblical Vice and Virtue Lists

Formal vice and virtue lists are found throughout the NT, sometimes in polysyndetic form (i.e., repetition of a conjunction [1 Cor. 6:9–10]) and sometimes in asyndetic form (i.e., no conjunction [Gal. 5:22–23]). Although some would include more and some fewer passages, the following texts generally are seen as representatives of this literary form in the NT:

Virtue Lists: 2 Cor. 6:6–7a; Gal. 5:22–23; Eph. 4:2–3, 31–5:2, 9; Phil. 4:8;
  Col. 3:12; 1 Tim. 3:2–4, 8–10, 11–12; 4:12; 6:11, 18; 2 Tim. 2:22–25; 3:10;
  Titus 1:8; 2:2–10; Heb. 7:26; 1 Pet. 3:8; 2 Pet. 1:5–7 (cf. Matt. 5:3–11;
  1 Cor. 13:4–7; Jas. 3:17)

Vice Lists: Matt. 15:19; Mark 7:21–22; Luke 18:11; Rom. 1:29–31; 13:13;
  1 Cor. 5:10–11; 6:9–10; 2 Cor. 12:20–21; Gal. 5:19–21; Eph. 4:31; 5:3–5;
  Col. 3:5–9; 1 Tim. 1:9–10; 6:4–5; 2 Tim. 3:2–4; Titus 1:7; 3:3; 1 Pet. 2:1;
  4:3, 15; Rev. 9:21; 21:8; 22:15 (cf. Luke 18:11)

These ethical catalogs perform a variety of rhetorical functions in the NT
writings. Some vice lists highlight the depravity of humanity in general (Matt.
15:19; Mark 7:21–22; Rom. 1:29–31; 1 Tim. 1:9–10), while others emphasize
or establish ethical boundaries between inheritors of the kingdom of God
and "the immoral of this world," as Paul puts it in 1 Cor. 5:10–11 (cf. Rom.
13:13; 1 Cor. 6:9–10; Eph. 5:3–5; Col. 3:5–9; 1 Pet. 4:3, 15). Several ethical lists
serve to encourage virtuous behavior by exhorting readers to exhibit certain
general qualities (Phil. 4:8; 1 Pet. 2:1; 3:8) or by reminding believers of the
characteristics of their old lives in contrast to the new existence that they
have in Christ (2 Cor. 12:20–21; Gal. 5:19–23; Eph. 4:31; Col. 3:12; Titus 3:3;
2 Pet. 1:5–7). Thus, the call to "clothe yourselves with compassion, kindness,
humility, meekness, and patience" (Col. 3:12b) is immediately preceded by a
reminder of the new identity that God's chosen saints have received in Christ
(Col. 3:11–12a). Particularly in the Pastoral Epistles, which contain the highest
concentration of ethical lists in the NT, the focus of virtue and vice catalogs is
on identifying qualities appropriate for ecclesiastical leaders (1 Tim. 3:1–12;
4:12; 6:11, 18–19; 2 Tim. 2:22–25; 3:10; Titus 1:7; 2:2–10 [cf. 2 Cor. 6:6–7a])
while at the same time denouncing as immoral the false teachers who are opposed in the letters (1 Tim. 6:3–5; 2 Tim. 3:2–4 [cf. Rev. 9:21; 21:8; 22:15]).
The virtue list in Heb. 7:26 ("For it was fitting that we should have such a high
priest, holy, blameless, undefiled, separated from sinners, and exalted above
the heavens") is distinctive in that it is primarily christological in nature.

The biblical vice lists, combined with the continuing influence of Platonic
and Aristotelian philosophical reflection on the nature of virtue and vice,
led to fertile contemplation of virtue and vice among Christian writers of
the patristic and medieval periods. Augustine (354–430), for example, emu-
lated his teacher Ambrose (339–97) in adding to the four cardinal virtues in
pagan thought (wisdom, temperance, justice, courage) three distinctively
theological virtues taken from 1 Cor. 13:13: faith, hope, and love (see *Mor.
eccl.* 15.25; cf. 1 Thess. 1:3; 5:8). For Augustine, the four classical virtues of

Greek philosophy are simply expressions of the highest Christian virtue, namely, love. The Christian tradition of the "seven deadly sins," well represented in Chaucer's *Parson's Tale*, has its origins in pastoral considerations of vice offered by writers such as John Cassian (ca. 360–435) and Pope Gregory the Great (ca. 540–604). In the modern period, an emphasis on natural law within Catholic theology and the rejection of the stress on virtue among nineteenth-century liberal Protestantism by Karl Barth and other neoorthodox theologians led to a turn away from virtue as a key theme of Christian ethics. Yet, with a renewed awareness of virtue ethics among Protestant theologians after Alasdair MacIntyre's groundbreaking work and in response to Stanley Hauerwas's ethical proposals, and with an increased interest in integrating Scripture more deeply into the rich tradition of moral theology among Catholics (especially after Vatican II's *Optatam totius* 16), the virtue and vice lists in the NT, along with the philosophical strands on which they draw, should once again spark reflection on the importance of character in the formation of Christian communities.

Bibliography

Aune, D. *The New Testament in Its Literary Environment*. Westminster, 1987.

Charles, J. *Virtue amidst Vice: The Catalog of Virtues in 2 Peter 1*. JSNTSup 150. Sheffield Academic Press, 1997.

Colish, M. *The Stoic Tradition from Antiquity to the Early Middle Ages*. 2 vols. SHCT 34–35. Brill, 1990.

Harrington, D., and J. Keenan. *Jesus and Virtue Ethics: Building Bridges between New Testament Studies and Moral Theology*. Sheed & Ward, 2002.

MacIntyre, A. *After Virtue: A Study in Moral Theory*. 3rd ed. University of Notre Dame Press, 2007.

McEleney, N. "The Vice Lists of the Pastoral Epistles." *CBQ* 36 (1974): 203–19.

✦ Love Command ✦

Thomas W. Ogletree

The Scriptures contain diverse yet mutually enriching perspectives on the love commands. These perspectives reflect a range of diverse social contexts, from Deuteronomy's comprehensive social construction of Israel's covenant legacy to Paul's counsel for marginal faith communities in an alien social environment.

Love Commands in the Old Testament

Deuteronomy displays the grounding of Israel's covenant calling in God's unrelenting love for his people and in his summons for them to love him in return (Deut. 4:35–39). A pivotal text is Deut. 6:4–5: "Hear, O Israel: The Lord is our God, the Lord alone. You shall love the Lord your God with all your heart, and with all your soul, and with all your might." The Hebrew word for "heart" has cognitive and volitional connotations, embracing "heart" and "mind"; "soul" suggests the depths of the self, and "might" expresses the full investment of our energies.

Building on the Ten Commandments, Deuteronomy provides an extensive list of statutes, laws, and ordinances that specify the requisites of social and political order, including a virtual constitution that establishes a division of powers between executive, legislative, and judicial processes designed to hold monarchs accountable to covenant standards (Deut. 17). Deuteronomy repeatedly stresses God's love for his people, including strangers living among them (Deut. 10:15, 18–19; 30:3), and it calls for heartfelt commitments by the people to uphold covenant faithfulness (Deut. 10:12–13, 16, 18–19; 11:13, 16, 18; 13:3; 26:16; 30:2, 10, 16). These themes reflect Jeremiah's vision of a new covenant that the Lord will engrave on the hearts of his people (Jer. 31:33–34) and Ezekiel's declaration that the Lord will give his people new hearts of flesh more responsive to his Spirit (Ezek. 36:26–27). Leviticus is the original source of the commands to love neighbors and resident aliens in the same way as one loves oneself (Lev. 19:18, 34). These commands are integrated with ritual observances and holiness codes designed to sustain the distinctive identity of the people of Israel. Neighbors are fellow members of the people of Israel, and aliens are to be welcomed as citizens, for the people of Israel survived as aliens in the land of Egypt.

Love Commands in the Synoptic Gospels

The Synoptic Gospels emphasize the unity of the commands to love both God and neighbor, though they represent these commands in distinctive ways. In Mark's narrative a scribe asks Jesus which commandment is first of all. Jesus responds by citing the command to love God with heart (*kardia*), soul (*psychē*), mind (*dianoia*), and strength (*ischys*), using four Greek terms in order to capture the richness of the Hebrew word for "heart" (Mark 12:30). Luke retains the same four terms, but Matthew omits the reference to "strength." Jesus then names a second command: love your neighbor as you love yourself. The scribe affirms Jesus' words, declaring that these commands are more important than burnt offerings and sacrifices (Mark 12:28–34). The scribe's observations are reinforced in Matthew's citation of Jesus' contention that ritual practices must not take precedence over "weightier matters of the law: justice and mercy and faith," words that capture the prophetic substance of Jesus' teachings (Matt. 23:23).

In Matthew's version of this exchange Jesus declares that all of the law and the prophets depend on the two Great Commandments (Matt. 22:34–40). This statement illumines his earlier claim that he had not come to abolish the law but rather to fulfill it, so that "not one letter, not one stroke of a letter, will pass from the law until all is accomplished" (Matt. 5:18). As the Sermon on the Mount makes clear, Jesus' reading of the law and the prophets is by no means focused on legalistic details, nor did he offer a comprehensive reading of the Ten Commandments. Instead, he provided a model for critical reflection on the moral substance of the law, one that emphasizes the importance of our feelings, needs, and desires and also our concrete interactions with our fellow human beings. Jesus suggests that explosive anger, harmful insults, lustful gazing, and deceitful oaths violate the underlying spirit of commands that prohibit murder, adultery, and a false witness against a neighbor. He urges his followers to take concrete steps to address these deeper problems, especially to seek ways of rebuilding broken relationships (Matt. 5:21–37) (see Stassen and Gushee 125–48).

Jesus also cites the Golden Rule: "In everything do to others as you would have them do to you," a rule that in Matthew he explicitly links to "the law and the prophets" (Matt. 7:12 [cf. Luke 8:31]). Jesus' teachings on the law are fully compatible with the spirit of Deuteronomy, which summons us to embrace God's commands in our hearts. In the Sermon on the Mount Jesus expands the reach of commands to love neighbors and strangers by urging us to love even our enemies and persecutors (Matt. 5:43–48; cf. Rom. 12:14–21). These words have inspired bold initiatives in peacemaking, conflict resolution, and restorative justice (see Cahill; Shriver; Stassen).

Jesus further challenges his followers to rise above the law of retribution, a law that mandates punishments for evildoers equivalent to the harm that they have caused. He directs special attention to the abusive practices of persons who wield power over others, and he calls for creative and potentially life-transforming moral responses to those practices: when someone strikes you on the right cheek, turn the other as well; when someone sues you for your coat, surrender your cloak as well; and if someone forces you to go one mile, go a second as well (Matt. 5:38–42). We are encouraged to accommodate such demands but to do so in ways that expose their lack of moral legitimacy (see Stassen and Gushee; Wink).

Luke places Jesus' discussion of the love commands in the context of his journey to Jerusalem, associating them with his broader Galilean mission (Luke 10.25–37). A lawyer stands up to test Jesus, asking what he must do to inherit eternal life. Jesus asks the lawyer how he read the law. The lawyer names the two Great Commandments, essentially describing them as one. Jesus assures the lawyer that by observing these commands he will live. The lawyer then asks, "Who is my neighbor?" Jesus responds by telling the parable of the good Samaritan. A priest and then a Levite walked past a man who had been seriously injured by thieves. A Samaritan showed him compassion, offering direct aid, taking him to an inn, and providing financial resources for his care. Jesus asks the lawyer which of the three men had been a neighbor to the victim, and the lawyer names the one who showed compassion. The parable does not explain who qualifies as a bona fide neighbor; instead, it discloses how good neighbors act. This parable has received special attention because it conveys an obligation to offer care as we are able for any and all of our fellow human beings, including strangers, enemies, and persecutors. Neighbor love becomes a universal principle that informs all aspects of our lives (see Nygren; Outka; Santurri and Werpehowski; Vacek).

Love Commands in the Gospel of John

The Gospel of John offers a christological transfiguration of the love commands. It begins with a declaration of God's love for the world, a love manifest in the gift of his only begotten Son (John 3:16). Jesus' own teachings on love are elaborated in his final conversations with his disciples as he prepares them to continue his mission. He begins by declaring his oneness with the heavenly Father. Those who believe in him believe in the Father, who sent him into the world (John 12:44); those who see him see the Father, who sent him as light into the world (John 12:46); those who hear him hear the words of the Father, who commands him to speak (John 12:49). He summarizes these claims by stating, "I am in the Father and the Father is in me" (John 14:10), a reality manifest in his good works.

Jesus then stresses his unity with his disciples, assuring them that he will not leave them desolate, even when the world no longer sees him. "You will see me," he promises them, and "because I live, you also will live" (John 14:19). "On that day you will know that I am in my Father, and you in me, and I in you" (John 14:20), for "the Father himself loves you, because you have loved me" (John 16:27). Jesus urges them to abide in him and in his love just as branches abide in a vine. They will then bear much fruit, and they will glorify the Father, though without him they can do nothing (John 15:1–11).

In the context of these conversations Jesus delivers a "new commandment": "Love one another just as I have loved you"; by practicing such love, they will be known as his disciples (John 13:34–35). Jesus' self-giving love now replaces traditional references to self-love as the standard for mutual love among his followers. Jesus observes that there is no greater love than a readiness to "lay down one's life for one's friends" (John 15:13). Jesus further states that he will no longer call his followers "servants" (*douloi*), for now they have become his friends (*philoi*) (John 15:15). The reference to friends explains why the Greek word for "love among friends," *philia*, sometimes appears in the Gospel of John alongside the more common NT term for "love," *agapē*. Jesus calls his followers "friends" because he has made known to them all that he has received from the Father (John 15:15). He promises that the Father will send them "another Advocate," the Holy Spirit, after he has departed from them (John 14:16). The Spirit will teach them all things, guide them into the truth, and refresh their memories about all that he has said to them (John 14:26). Empowered by the Spirit, they will do not only the works that he has done but also even greater works by continuing to abide in his love (John 14:12). They will keep his commandments, and the Father will love them (John 14:21). Jesus reminds his followers that the world will hate them just as it has hated him (John 15:18–25), for servants are not greater than their master. Even though the world's hatred has no legitimate cause, people who kill Jesus' followers may still believe that they are serving God (John 15:18–25; 16:2). These words prepared Jesus' followers for times of suffering and persecution.

Finally, in his private prayers Jesus states that he is praying not for the world but rather for those whom the Father has given him. They belong to the Father because they are the ones through whom he will be glorified (John 17:9–10). The Gospel of John characterizes Jesus' own crucifixion as his glorification (John 17:1–5). By enduring the world's hatred, Jesus' friends will be glorified as well—a message that parallels Jesus' words of blessing for the persecuted in his Sermon on the Mount (Matt. 5:11–12). Jesus also prays for those who will come to believe in him through the testimonies of his friends (John 17:20). Earlier he had spoken of "other sheep" not of his fold, sheep that he would gather into one flock with one shepherd—an apparent reference to gentile converts (John 10:16). Jesus prays that those who believe in him will become perfectly one, just as he and the Father are one (John 17:21–22), which underscores the urgency of communal solidarity for those who continue Jesus' mission. Their bonds will disclose to the world the truth that the Father sent them into the world, and that he loves the world just as he loves his only Son (John 17:23–26).

Epistles attributed to John reiterate many of these themes, stressing mutual love, caring responses to brothers and sisters in Christ who are in need, and a resolve to abide in the love of God (1 John 3:11–18, 23–24; 4:7–12, 16–21). Jesus' reference to the "new commandment" of mutual love (John 13:34) is qualified in 1 John, for this commandment has been disclosed from the beginning (1 John 2:7; cf. 2 John 4–6). The commandment is new in the sense that "the darkness is passing away and the true light is already shining" (1 John 2:8). The epistle adds, "Whoever loves a brother or sister lives in the light, and in such a person there is no cause for stumbling. But whoever hates another believer is in the darkness, walks in the darkness, and does not know the way to go, because the darkness has brought on blindness" (1 John 2:10–11).

Love Commands in the Letters of the New Testament

Paul's reading of the love commands is informed by his account of the Spirit of life in Jesus Christ. He makes no specific reference to the command to love God, giving central place to notions of faith, trust, and faithfulness. Even so, he does address his Corinthian readers as those who love God, citing multiple texts from Isaiah (1 Cor. 2:9; cf. Isa. 52:15; 64:4; 65:16). He also describes love for God as a sign that one is known by God (1 Cor. 8:3). Even the command to love neighbors is seldom mentioned, though Paul does state in his Letter to the Galatians, "The whole law is summed up in a single commandment, 'You shall love your neighbor as yourself'" (Gal. 5:14). He urges members of the Galatian community to become servants of one another lest they bite and devour one another (Gal. 5:15), and he calls for patience in addressing potentially divisive conflicts, for without such patience the church will not flourish.

Of central importance in Paul's letters are his persistent calls for mutual love within concrete faith communities, building upon the image of the church as the body of Christ. This message is introduced in 1 Cor. 12–13 and reiterated in Rom. 12. While different parts of the body have distinctive functions, Paul observes, they remain dependent upon one another as a condition of their effectiveness. In a similar manner, members of the body of Christ also have diverse gifts. There are apostles, prophets, teachers, healers, servants, leaders, and speakers in various tongues. All of these gifts can play roles in building up the body of Christ, but without love they become meaningless, even provoke divisions and conflicts within the body (1 Cor. 12:27–31; cf. Rom. 12:4–8). Paul especially emphasizes limitations in the gift of "speaking in tongues," for without an interpreter such speaking amounts to unintelligible noise (1 Cor. 14). Paul's central message is that members of the body must not compete with one another, still less foster conflicts that fragment the church. Instead, they must embrace one another in a love that is patient and kind, a love that "bears all things, believes all things, hopes all things, and endures all things" (1 Cor. 13:7). Faith, hope, and love are the enduring gifts of the Spirit, and love is the most important gift of all (1 Cor. 13:8–13). In his letter to the church in Rome Paul also calls for contributions to the "needs of the saints" and "hospitality to strangers" (Rom. 12:13).

Paul most clearly linked neighbor love to the fulfillment of the law in his Letter to the Romans. The text in Romans is distinctive in several ways. First, Paul's reference to the second love command follows his more general counsel regarding respect and honor for governing authorities (see Rom. 13:1–7). Second, he introduces his comments by emphasizing mutual love: "Owe no one anything, except to love one another" (Rom. 13:8). Third, he articulates the love command in two ways: initially as love for "another" (*ton heteron* [Rom. 13:8]) and subsequently as love for "the neighbor" (*ton plēsion* [Rom. 13:9]). Love for another conveys a love without limits, embracing all human beings, while love for neighbors directs attention to persons with whom we have ongoing relationships. Paul's language parallels the commands cited in Leviticus to love one's neighbors and to love resident aliens (Lev. 19:18, 34). Fourth, Paul states that by loving another we fulfill the law. He then lists selected mandates from the second table of the Ten Commandments: do not commit adultery, do not kill, do not steal, do not covet; he adds the phrase "and any other commandment," an apparent reference to commands similar in substance to those cited (Rom. 13:9–10). Read in context, Paul's words suggest parallels between the commands that he mentions and elements of Roman law, which he earlier identified as the law of the gentiles (Rom. 2:14–15). He does not refer to the first table of the Ten Commandments, for Rome could not be trusted to prevent idolatry, restrain vain religious expressions, or honor the Sabbath.

Given Paul's claims that Christ is the end of the law (Rom. 10:4), and that the law of the Spirit of life in Christ has replaced the old written code (Rom. 7:6), how could he also speak of mutual love, love for another, and neighbor love as fulfilling the law? Paul's purpose here is to assure his readers that the law did have continuing importance for sustaining social order, and that Roman authorities bore responsibility for enforcing the law. In so doing, they were not a terror to good conduct, but only to what is bad. Thus, Rom. 12–13 dramatizes fundamental differences between life within churches and respect for governing authorities. At the same time, Paul urges the faithful to extend the love that formed their life in Christ into the wider social world, offering blessings to those who persecuted them, refusing to repay anyone evil for evil, and renouncing vengeance—principles that echo Jesus' teachings in the Sermon on the Mount. He further calls them to provide food and drink for enemies who are hungry or thirsty. They must never be "overcome with evil," but rather they must "overcome evil with good" (Rom. 12:14–21).

Other epistles in the NT reinforce teachings on the love commands in the Synoptic Gospels and the Pauline Epistles. The Epistle of James displays connections between Matthew's treatment of the enduring authority of the law and Paul's references to freedom from the law in Christ Jesus. "Show me your faith apart from your works," James declares, "and I by my works will show you my faith" (Jas. 2:18). Faith without works, James insists, is "barren," even "dead" (Jas. 2:17, 20, 26). Citing Lev. 19:18, James further insists that by loving our neighbors we fulfill the law (Jas. 2:8). This epistle especially condemns acts of favoritism toward the wealthy and neglect for those in need (Jas. 2:1–7), and it stresses the urgency of addressing internal conflicts within faith communities (Jas. 4:1–3). It calls for "wisdom from above" that is "peaceable, gentle, willing to yield, full of mercy" (Jas. 3:13–17). First Peter reiterates Paul's emphasis on mutual love and the sharing of gifts within faith communities (1 Pet. 1:22–23; 4:7–11), and it combines calls for "unity of spirit" (1 Pet. 3:8) within the body of believers with appeals to show regard for governing authorities (1 Pet. 2:13–17). Second Peter lists virtues that reflect Paul's account of the fruit of the Spirit (2 Pet. 1:5–7).

Conclusions

The love commands disclose the roots of substantive moral teachings in God's compassionate love. Human beings are summoned not simply to submit to God's dominion, but to love God passionately in return. Special attention is given to communal solidarity among people who have a distinctive calling within God's larger purposes, including the people of Israel and a new people of God taking form in Jesus Christ. Communal solidarity does not imply closed communities but rather underscores the social bonds essential for sustaining a wider mission. These communities also were expected to remain open to others, welcoming "strangers" and "aliens" into their common life. In Jesus' Sermon on the Mount and in Paul's letter to the Romans the faithful are further summoned to extend practices of mutual love into the wider social world, embracing even their enemies and persecutors. Thus, neighbor love entails commitments to peacemaking and conflict resolution, fostering more constructive relationships among people who have been formed by diverse social and cultural practices. Such initiatives exemplify the universal scope of the love commands.

Bibliography

Cahill, L. *Love Your Enemies: Discipleship, Pacifism, and Just War Theory.* Fortress, 1994.

Furnish, V. *The Love Command in the New Testament.* Abingdon, 1972.

Nygren, A. *Agape and Eros.* Trans. P. Watson. University of Chicago Press, 1982 [1953].

Outka, G. *Agape: An Ethical Analysis.* Yale University Press, 1972.

Santurri, E., and W. Werpehowski, eds. *The Love Commandments: Essays in Christian and Moral Philosophy.* Georgetown University Press, 1992.

Shriver, D., Jr. *An Ethic for Enemies: Forgiveness in Politics.* Oxford University Press, 1995.

Stassen, G. *Just Peacemaking: Ten Practices for Abolishing War.* Pilgrim Press, 1998.

———. *Just Peacemaking: Transformative Initiatives for Justice and Peace.* Westminster John Knox, 1992.

Stassen, G., and D. Gushee. *Kingdom Ethics: Following Jesus in Contemporary Contexts.* InterVarsity, 2003.

Vacek, E. *Love Human and Divine: The Heart of Christian Ethics.* Georgetown University Press, 1994.

Wink, W. *Violence and Nonviolence in South Africa: Jesus' Third Way.* New Society Publishers, 1987.

◆ Love of Enemy ◆

Sondra E. Wheeler

The word *enemy* most frequently translates *'ōyēb* in Hebrew, meaning "one who hates." In the NT, *echthros* is the only word translated "enemy," and it is the consistent choice in the LXX, where it occurs more than four hundred times. Not formally defined in the canon, *enemy* is interpreted by rhetorical or poetic parallel with phrases such as "those who hate us" or "those who persecute you." It is used of both personal and national enemies.

The love of enemies is both commanded and enacted by Jesus in the NT. The imperative is issued most famously in his Sermon on the Mount, where loving and praying for one's enemies is offered as the crucial form of imitation that makes one a child of the heavenly Father (Matt. 5:44–45; cf. Luke 6:27–28, 35). Among the traditional "seven last words" of Christ on the cross is the prayer, "Father, forgive them; for they know not what they are doing," recorded in some manuscripts of Luke's Gospel (23:34). The parable that we call "the parable of the good Samaritan" takes much of its point from the traditional animosity between Jews and Samaritans, making the inclusion of enemies as neighbors to be loved the force of Jesus' directive, "Go and do likewise" (Luke 10:37).

However, admonitions to love enemies are not limited to the Gospels or even to the NT. Paul's instructions for the treatment of enemies in Romans, "If your enemies are hungry, feed them; if they are thirsty, give them something to drink" (12:20), are taken directly from Proverbs (25:21–22), which addresses not only conduct toward enemies but also inward attitudes toward them: "Do not rejoice when your enemies fall, and do not let your heart be glad when they stumble" (24:17).

The general imperative is fleshed out in various stipulations of the law (e.g., "When you come upon your enemy's ox or donkey going astray, you shall bring it back" [Exod. 23:4]) and repeatedly shown in narrative—for example, the reconciliation between Esau and Jacob (Gen. 33:4); the reunion of Joseph with the brothers who had sold him into slavery (Gen. 45:5); the young girl stolen into slavery who advised that Naaman the Syrian go to Elisha to be healed of his leprosy (2 Kgs. 5:2).

Above all other instances is the example of God's own patient love for enemies, manifested not only in his ever-renewed mercy on unfaithful Israel but also in his readiness to embrace traditional rivals such as Egypt and Assyria (Isa. 19:18–25; Jonah). Finally, Christ died for us while we were yet sinners (Rom. 5:8), having made ourselves enemies of God. As forgiven and reconciled people, Christians are made ambassadors of God and are entrusted with the work of reconciliation exemplified in the practice of loving enemies. However, the scope of this practice and its implications for public and political life are perennially contested.

Bibliography

Cahill, L. *Love Your Enemies: Discipleship, Pacifism, and Just War Theory*. Fortress, 1994.

Jones, L. *Embodying Forgiveness: A Theological Analysis*. Eerdmans, 1996.

Stassen, G. *Just Peacemaking: Transforming Initiatives for Justice and Peace*. Westminster John Knox, 1992.

Yoder, J. *The Politics of Jesus: Vicit Agnus Noster*. 2nd ed. Eerdmans, 1994.

◆ Love of Neighbor ◆
Nijay K. Gupta

Loving one's neighbor is central to Jewish and Christian ethics. The context within which this command comes is the Holiness Code of Leviticus: "You shall not take vengeance or bear a grudge against any of your people, but you shall love your neighbor as yourself: I am the LORD" (19:18). Although the importance that Christians place on this injunction is clear, the exact meaning of the text is less so. A proper theological and ethical interpretation of the command to love one's "neighbor" as oneself must deal with three questions: What does "neighbor" mean? What does it mean to "love" the neighbor? And what does it mean to love the neighbor "as yourself"?

Attending to Scripture and Early Jewish Conceptions

Neighbor

In the OT, the Hebrew word often translated as "neighbor" (*rēaʿ*) primarily involves some form of closeness, whether physical (Exod. 11:2; Judg. 6:29), social (Prov. 19:6), or ethnic (Exod. 2:13). There is good reason to understand *rēaʿ* in Lev. 19:18 as pertaining to the neighbor who is related by virtue of the covenant. Although this would naturally focus the view on loving (primarily) other Israelites, the discussion just prior to 19:18 involves more specifically care for the "poor and the alien" (19:10), as well as the deaf and the blind (19:14).

Even though Lev. 19:18 centers on loving within the community (and addressed outsiders only insofar as treatment of resident aliens was fair), the meaning of neighbor as kin (see "kin" in 19:17) was galvanized and treated by some as a command to avoid improper associations in early Judaism. Ben Sira observes that it is natural and proper to associate with one's own kind, to love your own "neighbor" (Sir. 13:15 [Gk. *plēsion*]). Allying with the wrong kinds of people is an abomination. Jesus criticizes the interpretation of Lev. 19:18 that exaggerates this bifurcation by seeing love of neighbor as promoting hatred toward enemies (Matt. 5:43). Enemies should be loved and treated as objects of prayer. Indeed, in Luke 10:25–37 Jesus turns a discussion about how to *identify* a neighbor into one about how to *be* a loving neighbor—that is, showing mercy and compassion to anyone in need, despite social and ethnic distance.

Love

In the Levitical context, loving is not simply an emotion; rather, it is characterized by doing the opposite of the preceding prohibitions in Lev. 19:10–17: looking after the needy, showing generosity toward laborers, having compassion for people with disabilities. The nature of these prohibitions reflects a working out of the Ten Commandments as a model for covenantal obedience with regard to the treatment of others. In the NT, Jesus commanded his disciples to love one another as he demonstrated love for them (John 15:12). The kind of love that Jesus gave is understood as a commitment to the other that may even lead to death (John 10:15; Eph. 5:2; 1 John 3:14).

Paul encouraged pleasing one's neighbors to strengthen them and to tolerate any inconveniences (Rom. 15:1–3). More radically, he described neighbor love as a disposition similar to being a slave to another person (Gal. 5:13–14). Similarly, James calls Lev. 19:18 the "royal law" that particularly discourages prejudice against the poor (Jas. 2:1–13).

As Yourself

The part of Lev. 19:18 that adds "as yourself" to the idea of loving the neighbor is open to several interpretations, but the most likely one has two aspects. The first involves seeking the highest good for the other as one naturally pursues what is best for oneself. The second is that Israelites should treat (and love) one another in the same way that they expect to be treated as ones who were equally made in God's likeness and who were equally freed by God from Egypt (see *Sipre Qodashim* 4.12).

In the Synoptic Gospels, Jesus encourages self-denial as a prerequisite for obedience (Matt. 16:24; Mark 8:34; Luke 9:23). Jesus is not promoting self-neglect here, though, but rather prioritizing the needs of others at a great cost to self. This is similarly expressed by Paul when he discourages the Philippians from working for selfish gain or pride (Phil. 2:3–4).

Ethical Implications

Two elements of the foregoing discussion are especially relevant to modern ethical discussions, one individual and one political. As for the former, picking up again the discussion of the role of "self" in loving the neighbor, it is commonly debated what relationship "I" have to "you" or "them." Garth Hallett outlines and assesses six models of Christ's "neighbor-love": self-preference, parity (i.e., equal benefit), other-preference, self-subordination, self-forgetfulness, and self-denial. Of these, he reasons that the most faithful model to the Christian tradition is self-subordination, which does not take the route of the last two models, which refrain from seeking one's own benefit at all. Instead, self-subordination allows for the consideration of one's own benefit, but it must never be to the disadvantage of another. The personal good can be sought out if that benefit could not be passed on to another or if another would not be limited or adversely affected in any way because of it. If one is inclined to agree with Hallett, Lev. 19:18 resists the idea that one loves the other and cannot seek out a happy life for oneself. This is particularly relevant to those who promote an ethic in which personal mistreatment and abuse should not be opposed.

The political aspect of neighbor love involves the problem of violence and warfare. Although a number of scriptural texts and theological issues are often brought to bear on this subject, it at least involves the basic concerns of love for neighbor and love for enemies. Does love for enemies exclude the physical resistance of them for a just cause? Does love for neighbor as a scriptural ideal mark out the church as a peaceable community that imitates Christ's humility and his refusal to act according to the vengeful and retributive nature of the fallen world? Although the basic moral thrust of the biblical idea of neighbor love is perspicuous, its application on this issue is more opaque.

Conclusion

To borrow and rework a well-known metaphor, the command "Love thy neighbor" is like an ocean: shallow enough that almost anyone can grasp its basic meaning, yet deep enough that its moral implications and applications are nearly bottomless. It stands within the heritage of Christianity as not just one of the two great love commandments affirmed by Jesus, but the necessary complement to the ideal of loving God. However one interprets this command to love of neighbor ethically, the struggle undoubtedly is over the center of the moral vision of the Bible itself.

Bibliography

Cahill, L. *Love Your Enemies: Discipleship, Pacifism, and Just War Theory*. Fortress, 1994.

Furnish, V. *The Love Command in the New Testament*. Abingdon, 1972.

Goldingay, J. *Israel's Life*. InterVarsity, 2009.

Gorman, M. *Cruciformity: Paul's Narrative Spirituality of the Cross*. Eerdmans, 2001.

Hallett, G. *Christian Neighbor-Love: An Assessment of Six Rival Versions*. Georgetown University Press, 1989.

Hays, R. *The Moral Vision of the New Testament: Community, Cross, and New Creation; A Contemporary Introduction to New Testament Ethics*. HarperSanFrancisco, 1996.

Milgrom, J. *Leviticus 17–22*. AB 3A. Doubleday, 2000.

Perkins, P. *Love Commands in the New Testament*. Paulist Press, 1982.

Swartley, W., ed. *The Love of Enemy and Nonretaliation in the New Testament*. Westminster John Knox, 1992.

◆ Sermon on the Mount ◆

Glen H. Stassen

The Sermon on the Mount (Matt. 5:1–7:12) is the largest block of Jesus' teaching in the NT and the most frequently referred to teaching in the church's early centuries (Kissinger 6). Surely, Jesus' Great Commission (Matt. 28:19–20), calling us to make disciples and teach them "to obey everything that I have commanded you," especially includes these teachings.

Ways of Interpreting that Lead to Evasion

Yet something is wrong. Harvey McArthur shows an enormous amount of rationalizing, evading, and accommodating in the usual ways of interpreting the Sermon on the Mount:

1. *Literal interpretation applied universally and absolutely.* Love is nonviolent, sacrificial, self-emptying, dying to self and rising to walk in newness of life, practicing servanthood in community. But many interpret the sermon idealistically: never be angry, never resist evil, merely allow whatever injustice is done to us. This strikes people as impossible in real life, so they call it "hard teachings" and devise ways to evade Jesus' teachings.

2. *Hyperbole.* Clearly Jesus uses hyperbole in Matt. 5:29: "If your right eye causes you to sin, tear it out and throw it away." But this applies only to the passages that are hyperboles. It is no excuse for watering down and rationalizing away the sermon, which is intended quite directly and seriously.

3. *General principles.* Surely, "Go also the second mile" applies to our context even if no Roman soldier requires us to carry his pack one mile. Therefore, many derive principles from what Jesus teaches concretely and apply them to today's context. But human nature often dilutes Jesus' command into a vague principle that loses its concrete meaning. A historically concrete hermeneutic will see Jesus' teachings in their full historical concreteness, anti-Roman hostility and all, without reducing them to a thin principle, and will carry the full concrete story over to our present situation, letting it take concrete shape in our historical context, with our own particular hostilities.

4. *Double standard.* As Constantinian Christianity compromised with the world, the notion developed that many of Jesus' teachings were only for monks who were seeking perfection, not for laypeople. Luther

criticized the medieval double-standard ethic severely but did not see how he could advocate not resisting evil. So he split public and secular life from inner and private life and said that in public life, "You do not have to ask Christ about your duty. Ask the imperial or the territorial law." Others have similarly split actions from attitudes and said that the sermon applies to attitudes but not to actions.

The result of these false splits was to block Jesus' teachings from real application and to render the gospel impotent in dealing with pogroms against Jews, the Holocaust, slavery, segregation, world hunger, economic injustice, and nuclear idolatry. It renders the public realm secularized, opens the door to rationalizing, and violates Jesus' first basic principle, which is that we are to serve God wholeheartedly and not money or other gods.

By contrast, the Sermon on the Mount splits those who actually do Jesus' commands and have their house built on the rock from those who do not do them and are headed to destruction. There is no third category for those who have good attitudes but do not do the teachings.

5. *Repentance.* This view considers the Sermon on the Mount, the Ten Commandments, and the ethical teachings of the Bible as law and opposes this to gospel. The Sermon on the Mount brings us to repentance because we cannot live up to it, but once we repent and accept forgiveness, we are free without the law, without actually doing what the sermon says.

This opens the door to a wide field of rationalizing and blocks the sermon from actually guiding our lives. Surely, the sermon does bring us to repentance when it is taken seriously, and the more we live by forgiveness, the more we can take the sermon seriously without flinching, even though we fail at times. Those who actually do these teachings have their house built on the rock (Matt. 7:16, 21, 24).

Peter Stuhlmacher points out that the NT throughout assumes the incumbency and practicality of the commands of Jesus; they are to be obeyed by Christians. Paul himself says that keeping the commands of God and obeying the law of Christ are essential for Christians (Rom. 8:3–8; 1 Cor. 7:19; 9:21; Gal. 6:2).

6. *Interim ethic* (Albert Schweitzer) and *dispensationalism* (J. N. Darby). Jesus expected the end of history to come very quickly and so intended his absolute love ethic only for the short interim before the end of history. We know, however, that history did not end that way, and so we have to fashion an ethic with more realism in it.

Or, we know that Jesus' ethic was intended for a future dispensation, an ideal world without sin, where there is peace, not for us in our time. For now, we need an ethic not based on Jesus' teaching that only those who do the will of God as Jesus teaches it enter the kingdom of heaven. Strangely, this agrees with the liberal Schweitzer that God's kingdom is not already at hand, already happening, but is totally future, and so we need to live by another ethic than that of Jesus.

But in fact the Sermon on the Mount is based on a realistic view of the world, where we know poverty, anger, murder, lust, idolatry, deceit, hate, hypocrisy, beams in our eyes, people taking each other to court and to severe punishment, judgment and self-righteousness, captivity to mammon (money), people not following the narrow path and going to their destruction. Where did anyone get the idea that Jesus was teaching only for an ideal world with no sin in it? He was teaching for a world that needs God's deliverance. God is already forgiving, already being merciful, already feeding the hungry, already speaking through Jesus, already shining his sun and sending his rain on the just and the unjust. Jesus nowhere said that his ethic was valid only if God would end the world soon. His ethic was based on God's nature, presence, and righteousness—a present reality.

The Sermon on the Mount as Transforming Initiatives of Deliverance

Until recently, the Sermon on the Mount usually was interpreted idealistically as antitheses, as if it prohibited being angry, lustful, and so on. Then it was seen as high ideals or hard teachings. So it was evaded, as noted above, or simply not preached or taught.

In fact, the structure of the Sermon on the Mount in Matt. 5:21–7:12 is not dyadic antitheses; rather, it is triadic transforming initiatives of proactive deliverance: not "hard teachings," but the way of deliverance. The consistent pattern is this: first, traditional righteousness; second, diagnosis of a vicious cycle; third, transforming initiatives that perform like mustard seeds of the reign of God breaking in.

Matthew 5:21–26 begins by citing the traditional righteousness, "You shall not murder." Second, Jesus diagnoses the vicious cycles of being angry and calling someone a fool. These are expressed in Greek participles diagnosing an ongoing practice. The NT gives no command against being angry; Jesus became angry at times (Matt. 21:12–13; 23; Mark 3:5). Third, Jesus commands us that when there is anger, we should go to our adversary and make peace. This is not a high-ideal prohibition but rather the realistic way of deliverance.

Matthew 5:27–30 begins with "You shall not commit adultery." The vicious cycle consists of looking at a woman with lust (expressed with a participle in the Greek text). Then comes the transforming initiative: "If your right eye causes you to sin, tear it out and throw it away." This is a dramatic exaggeration for impact, a hyperbole. I suggest that it means "Cut out the practice that is leading you to be looking with lust," such as meeting this woman secretly or looking at pornography.

Matthew 5:38–42 begins with the traditional teaching about retaliating with an eye for an eye. Then comes the diagnosis and proscription of the vicious cycle, which should be understood as "not to be retaliating revengefully by evil means." The apostle Paul also gives the teaching that way in Rom. 12:17–21. Translating Jesus' words in Matt. 5:39 as "Do not resist an evildoer" does not fit the Greek; does not fit Jesus' practice of resisting Pharisees, money changers, and Peter (Matt. 16:23); and misinterprets Jesus as teaching impossible ideals.

Then comes the climax, the four transforming initiatives. (1) Turning the other cheek is not merely complying with injustice. In Jewish culture, where there was no soap, it was forbidden to touch someone with your left hand, which was used for personal hygiene. So a right-handed slap on the right cheek was a backhanded insult, saying, "You dog! You nothing!" Turning the left cheek was turning the cheek of equal dignity. It was a nonviolent initiative confronting the injustice. (2) In biblical teaching, if you took someone's coat as collateral for a loan, you had to return it every night so that the owner had something warm to sleep in when it got cold. If a greedy person unjustly sues for the coat, and you give your cloak as well, you stand there naked, confronting the greed nonviolently, hoping that the embarrassment leads to repentance. (3) When the Roman soldier forces you to carry his pack one mile—a symbol of unjust foreign occupation—you go a second mile, probably conversing on the way as Matt. 5:21–26 suggests, nonviolently confronting the injustice. (4) When a beggar begs for money, thereby confronting you with your greed, give, but also lend. Jesus never teaches mere compliance with something that you are forced to do; he always teaches a nonviolent transforming initiative aimed at a relationship of justice and peacemaking.

Matthew 5:43–48 begins by relating a traditional teaching from the Dead Sea Scrolls: "You shall love your neighbor and hate your enemy." This vicious cycle fails to exceed the righteousness of the tax collectors and gentiles. The transforming initiative is to love your enemies and pray for your persecutors "so that you may be children of your heavenly Father," who includes the just and the unjust in his gift of sunshine and rain.

The sentence that climaxes the first six transforming initiatives in English translations is "Be perfect, therefore, as your heavenly Father is perfect" (Matt.

5:48). Idealism interprets this as a mandate to live up to high ideals. However, it makes no sense biblically to say "as your heavenly Father lives up to high ideals"; there is no ideal above God for God to live up to. Jesus is saying that God is complete or inclusive in love, giving sun and rain to the unjust as well as the just. What Jesus means is this: "Be complete (in your love), as your heavenly Father is complete in loving enemies." Luke 6:36 agrees: "Be merciful, just as your Father is merciful."

Matthew 5:21–7:12 follows this threefold pattern consistently for fourteen teachings, with one exception. (Note that Jesus' genealogy in Matt. 1:2–17 is three times fourteen generations, with one exception.) In all fourteen teachings the main verb in the first part is consistently a future or a subjunctive; the vicious cycle is always expressed with a continuous-action verb (participle, infinitive, or indicative); the transforming initiative is always expressed as an imperative, always an initiative of deliverance, never an idealistic prohibition. This much consistency surely is intentional: Jesus' teachings are grace-based transforming initiatives of deliverance, not idealistic antitheses.

The NRSV mistranslates Matt. 7:13–14 idealistically, as if Jesus teaches that the road is "easy" that leads to destruction, and the road is "hard" that leads to life. The Greek text, however, contrasts a wide road with a narrow road. Jesus says, "My yoke is easy, and my burden is light" (Matt. 11:30). A life of truthfulness, love, peace, and sobriety is actually an easier life than one of deceit, hate, violence, and drunkenness.

Bibliography

Allison, D. C., Jr. *Studies in Matthew: Interpretation Past and Present*. Baker Academic, 2005.

Carter, W. *What Are They Saying about Matthew's Sermon on the Mount?* Paulist Press, 1994.

Guelich, R. *The Sermon on the Mount: A Foundation for Understanding*. Word, 1982.

Hendrickx, H. *The Sermon on the Mount*. Rev. ed. Geoffrey Chapman, 1984.

Kissinger, W. *The Sermon on the Mount: A History of Interpretation and Bibliography*. Scarecrow Press, 1975.

Lapide, P. *The Sermon on the Mount: Utopia or Program for Action?* Trans. A. Swidler. Orbis, 1986.

McArthur, H. *Understanding the Sermon on the Mount*. Harper, 1960.

Stassen, G. "The Fourteen Triads of the Sermon on the Mount: Matthew 5:21–7:12." *JBL* 122 (2003): 267–308.

———. *Living the Sermon on the Mount: Practical Hope for Grace and Deliverance*. Jossey-Bass, 2006.

♦ Use of Parables in Ethics ♦

John R. Donahue

Paul offers an epitome of Christian ethics: "Live your life in a manner worthy of the gospel of Christ" (Phil. 1:27) and "Let the same mind be in you that was in Christ Jesus" (Phil. 2:5). Characteristic of the Gospels is that Jesus "began to teach them many things in parables" (Mark 4:2), and the parables have been and remain a rich resource for discipleship and ethical reflection. The challenge is to describe how they so function in the Gospels and how they can be continually appropriated.

Speaking in Parables

"Parable," from the Greek *parabolē*, entails placing things side by side for the sake of comparison. In the LXX, *parabolē* normally translates the Hebrew *māšāl*, which embraces various literary forms. Parables, then, would include proverbs (1 Sam. 10:12; Prov. 1:1, 6; 26:7–9), riddles (Judg. 14:10–18), taunt songs (Mic. 2:4; Hab. 2:6), oracles (Num. 23:7, 18), and metaphors and allegories (Isa. 5:1–7; Ezek. 17:2–24). In the Gospels, parabolic material includes proverbs (Luke 4:23), examples (Luke 12:16–21), similitudes (Luke 5:36–39), similes (Matt. 13:33), allegory (Matt. 25:1–13), as well as the more familiar narrative parables (Luke 10:25–37; 15:11–32).

The wide use of the term *parable* has spawned a major problem of interpretation of the nature and function of parables, with the distinction between parable and allegory occupying center stage. The word *allegory* (from Gk. *allēgoreō*, "to speak otherwise than one seems to speak") is defined as "description of a subject under the guise of some other subject of aptly suggestive resemblance" (*Oxford English Dictionary*). It has been applied to biblical passages such as Isa. 5:1–7, the infidelity of the people described as an unfruitful vineyard, or to a whole book, such as Song of Songs. In the NT itself, parables are interpreted as allegories (Matt. 13:36–43; Mark 4:13–20). Allegory quickly became a dominant characteristic of parable interpretation throughout church history. For example, in reflecting on the parable of the good Samaritan (Luke 10:29–37), Augustine identifies the man who went down from Jerusalem to Jericho as Adam; Jerusalem is the state of original happiness; Jericho represents human mortality; the Samaritan is Christ; the inn is the church; the innkeeper is Paul; and so on (Dodd 1–2). Allegory interprets details independent of their literary and historical context. It is also coded language for insiders that illustrates or supports the previously held beliefs of a definite group. Although the rejection of allegory became a keystone of parable interpretation, often there was a failure to distinguish between interpreting nonallegorical material in an allegorical manner and allegory as a vital literary genre. Fruitful interpretation can take place as well through an allegorical retelling of a parable that remains faithful to the originating meaning of the parable.

With the rise of historical criticism, allegorical interpretation fades, due especially to the influence of Adolf Jülicher, whose two-volume study marked a new era in parable research. From an understanding of *parabolē* as found in Greek rhetoric, Jülicher argued that parables were extended similes, whereas allegories were developed metaphors. In a simile, the point of comparison is clearly indicated by "like" or "as" (e.g., Luke 11:44), whereas metaphor is a compressed simile in which something is "transferred" or carried over (the literal meaning of *metapherō*) from one sphere to another, as in "The eye is the lamp of the body" (Matt. 6:22). Jülicher calls metaphor "inauthentic speech" that obscures rather than illustrates truth.

According to Jülicher, every parable is composed of an "image" (*Bild*) and the "reality part" (*Sache*), what the image points to. The focus of his position is that each parable has only one point of comparison. The individual details or characters in a parable have no meaning outside the parable (e.g., in Luke 15:11–32, the father does not stand for God, nor the elder brother for the Pharisees), and the point of comparison is one of the widest possible moral application.

Although subsequent scholarship rejected many of Jülicher's interpretations principally because of the rigidity of the single-point approach, the minimizing of OT background of Jesus' teaching, and the neglect of similarities between Jesus and early rabbinic teachers, Jülicher anticipated the major strains of parable research in the twentieth century: concern for parable as a literary form, parables as an entrée to kingdom proclamation, and, later, the self-understanding of Jesus, and the ethical relevance of parables.

The most influential interpreter of the parables in the twentieth century was Joachim Jeremias. With almost unparalleled knowledge of first-century Palestine, Jeremias sheds light on the details of daily life that provide the material for the parables. More significantly, he carefully analyzes the changes that the parables underwent as they moved from the setting in the life of Jesus through the missionary proclamation of the early church and to their final incorporation into the Gospels. For example, parables are allegorized (Matt. 13:36–43; Mark 4:14–20); parables addressed originally to opponents are directed to church leaders (Matt. 18:10–14; Luke 15:1–7); details are embellished; and OT allusions are added.

Jeremias's study of the parables, then, becomes a full-scale study of the message of Jesus. He rejected "realized eschatology," as advocated by C. H. Dodd, and proposed "inaugurating eschatology"—that is, in the process of realization. The definitive revelation of God's reign has begun in Jesus; its full effect lies in the future. Jeremias's view prevailed both as a faithful exegesis of Jesus' parables and of Christian eschatology in general.

Although Dodd did not stress the ethical implication of the parables beyond their urgent call to conversion, Jeremias sketched the major ethical demands of Jesus by grouping particular parables under headings such as "God's Mercy for Sinners," "It May Be Too Late," "The Challenge of the Hour," and "Realized Discipleship." Klyne Snodgrass adopts a similar approach in the most recent comprehensive study of the parables.

In the last third of the twentieth century, concern for the form and literary quality of the parables prevailed over their use to reconstruct the teaching of Jesus. Along with concern for the parables as the key to the teaching of Jesus, the other major focus of parable research has been concern for their literary nature. This owes much to Dodd's inductive description of parable "as a metaphor or simile drawn from nature or common life, arresting the hearer by its vividness or strangeness and leaving the mind in sufficient doubt about its precise application to tease it into active thought" (Dodd 5). These qualities of metaphoric language, realism, paradox, and open-ended summons to personal engagement became the focus for subsequent discussion.

Seminal works by Amos Wilder and Robert Funk viewed parables primarily as poetic rather than rhetorical forms where an appreciation of metaphor provided a key to a new vision of the parables. Metaphor, they noted, by the often surprising equation of dissimilar elements—for example, "You are the salt of the earth" (Matt. 5:13)—produces an impact on the imagination that cannot be conveyed by discursive speech. With Funk and Wilder, metaphor has moved from literary trope or figure to a theological and hermeneutical category; it is especially suited to express the two necessary qualities of all religious language, immediacy and transcendence. A religious experience, that sense of awe in the face of the holy or of being grasped by mystery, is immediate and personal and, in great religious literature, is expressed in concrete, physical imagery.

The parables of Jesus are more exactly "metaphoric" rather than metaphors, since metaphor involves the combination of two distinct images joined in a single sentence, whereas the Gospel parables generally are extended narratives. They combine narrative form and metaphoric process (Ricoeur). Focus quickly shifted to a "narrative" reading of parables. Again, Wilder was a leader. He argued that in telling about God's reign "in story," Jesus continued the narrative legacy of biblical revelation. In reading the stories of Jesus, a Christian realizes that life is "a race, a pilgrimage, in short, a story" (Wilder 65).

Ethics and the Parables

The formal characteristics of parables themselves have ethical implications. Jesus used realistic images from daily life that caught his hearers' attention by their vividness and narrative color. Yet his parables have a surprising twist; the realism is shattered, and the hearers knew that something more was at stake than a homey illustration to drive home a point. The parables raise questions, unsettle the complacent, and challenge the hearers to reflection and inquiry.

Illustrations from Daily Life

In the parables of Jesus the life of ordinary people from a distant time and culture comes alive in a way found rarely in ancient literature. Jesus was familiar with a rural Galilean milieu: outdoor scenes of farming and shepherding, and domestic scenes in a simple one-room house (Luke 11:5–8). Jesus sees life through the eyes of the *'ănāwîm*, the poor and humble of the land. This creates an obstacle for the modern urban reader and poses challenges to historians and archaeologists to help us understand better the cultural context of the parables. The realism of the parables means also that Jesus places the point of contact between God and humans within the everyday world of human experience. Jesus does not proclaim the kingdom in "God language"; rather, he summons his hearers to realize that their destinies are at stake in their "ordinary, creaturely existence, domestic, economic, social" (Wilder 82).

Novelty and Paradox

The realism of the parables is but one side of the coin. The novel twists in Jesus' stories make his hearers take notice. The harvest is not just bountiful, but extravagant (Mark 4:8); the mustard seed is the smallest of seeds, yet it becomes the "greatest of all shrubs" (Mark 4:31–32). The vineyard owner paying first those hired last (Matt. 20:8) makes the reader suspect that something strange is about to happen. A major key to the "meaning" of a given parable appears when the realism begins to break down.

Parables express a paradox, a seeming absurdity that conceals a deeper truth. Their fundamental message is that things are not as they seem; you must have your tidy image of reality shattered. The good Samaritan is not primarily an illustration of compassion and loving-kindness to the suffering, but rather a challenge to see as good those whom we would call enemy. The strange and paradoxical character of the parables is a counterpart to Jesus' association with, and offer of mercy and grace to, tax collectors and sinners, those thought to be beyond the pale of God's concern. Similarly, Paul Ricoeur notes that parables operate in a pattern of orientation, disorientation, and reorientation. Their hyperbolic and paradoxical language presents an extravagance that interrupts our normal way of viewing things and presents the extraordinary within the ordinary. The parables dislocate our project of trying to make a tight pattern of our lives, which Ricoeur feels is akin to the Pauline "boasting" or justification by works.

An Open-Ended Challenge

In their transmission the parables received different applications and interpretations. Appended to the enigmatic parable of the unjust steward is a parade of interpretations, joined mainly by catchwords (Luke 16:8b–13). Other parables have appended sayings that are found in a number of different contexts (e.g., Matt. 25:13 = Mark 13:35; Matt. 25:29 = Mark 4:25; Matt. 13:12; Luke 8:18). The audience shifts; parables originally addressed to opponents are directed to the church (Matt. 18:1, 12–14; Luke 15:2–7). In their original form, the parables of Jesus may have ended at the narrative conclusion (e.g., Matt. 13:30; 18:34) or with a question or challenge (e.g., Matt. 20:15; 21:31; Mark 4:9). The meaning of a given parable often is elusive: is the point of the parable of the pearl (Matt. 13:45–46) the search, the joy of finding, or the willingness to risk all? Both in the early church and in subsequent history, the parables are "polyvalent." They demand and receive different interpretation from different audiences. Although exegesis may determine the parameters of misinterpretation of a given parable, it can scarcely exhaust the potentialities for fruitful interpretation and application.

Parables are open-ended; they are invitations waiting for a response. The parable does not really exist until it is freely appropriated. The response of the reader or hearer in a real sense creates the meaning of the parable. Parable is a form of religious discourse that appeals not only to the imagination or to the joyous perception of paradox or surprise but also to the most basic of human qualities, freedom. Jesus chose a form of discourse that put his life and message at the risk of free human response.

Appropriating the parables for Christian ethics is an aspect of the larger issue of the relation of Scripture and ethics. Fundamentally, the parables are an aspect of "remembering Jesus," and through preaching and study they form the conscience of Christian communities (Verhey 22–26; 286–87). The parables provide a storehouse of images that counter distorted images flooding our consciousness (Spohn 60–64). The poor, the disabled, and marginal are not to be hidden or neglected but are to be welcomed for dinner (Luke 14:16–24); women are not to be seen as powerless victims when a widow claims her rights before a corrupt judge (Luke 18:1–8); remembering Jesus is to follow the trajectory of the church through the ages as it retells and adapts the parables of Jesus.

Parables likewise contain clear exhortations to discipleship, warnings about failure, examples of virtues and vices; they nurture Christian attitudes and dispositions and enrich the imagination of believers. Although from a cultural milieu strange to most people today, they have a universal quality that, through reflective analogy, can shape the values of a Christian community. Experiencing and extending forgiveness "from one's heart" is a fundamental Christian challenge (Matt. 18:23–35), and the claims of justice should not limit generosity (Matt. 20:1–16). Christians still long for a God who reaches out in a surprising manner to the prodigal and the dutiful and risks the good of the majority to seek out the lost (Luke 15:1–32); blindness to the destitute at one's doorstep is a stain on Christian faith (Luke 16:19–31). The shock that the threatening outsider can actually be a "good Samaritan" who heals and gives life can overturn fixed prejudices and correct false values (Luke 10:25–37). The Gospels continue to teach many things in parables.

Bibliography

Blomberg, C. *Interpreting the Parables.* InterVarsity, 1992.

Dodd, C. H. *The Parables of the Kingdom.* Charles Scribner's Sons, 1961.

Donahue, J. *The Gospel in Parable: Metaphor, Narrative, and Theology in the Synoptic Gospels.* Fortress, 1988.

Funk, R. *Language, Hermeneutic, and the Word of God: The Problem of Language in the New Testament and Contemporary Theology.* Harper & Row, 1966.

Hultgren, A. *The Parables of Jesus: A Commentary.* Eerdmans, 2002.

Jeremias, J. *The Parables of Jesus.* Trans. S. Hooke. Scribner, 1972.

Jülicher, A. *Die Gleichnisreden Jesu.* 2 vols. Wissenschaftliche Buchgesellschaft, 1969 [1899].

Kissinger, W. *The Parables of Jesus: A History of Interpretation and Bibliography.* Scarecrow Press and American Library Association, 1979.

Perrin, N. *Jesus and the Language of the Kingdom: Symbol and Metaphor in New Testament Interpretation.* Fortress, 1976.

Ricoeur, P. "Biblical Hermeneutics." *Semeia* 4 (1975): 27–148.

Scott, B. *Hear Then the Parable: A Commentary on the Parables of Jesus.* Fortress, 1989.

Snodgrass, K. *Stories with Intent: A Comprehensive Guide to the Parables of Jesus.* Eerdmans, 2008.

Spohn, W. *Go and Do Likewise: Jesus and Ethics.* Continuum, 1999.

Verhey, A. *Remembering Jesus: Christian Community, Scripture, and the Moral Life.* Eerdmans, 2002.

Wilder, A. *Early Christian Rhetoric: The Language of the Gospel.* Harvard University Press, 1972.

6

⫫⫫

BEYOND THE NEW
TESTAMENT

♦ Apostolic Fathers ♦

Clayton N. Jefford

The Apostolic Fathers is a collection of late-first- to mid-second-century texts that form a bridge between the NT and patristic literature. Typically included are the following: a letter by the church at Rome (*1 Clement*), a letter by Polycarp of Smyrna (*To the Philippians*) and an account of his martyrdom (*Martyrdom of Polycarp*), seven letters by Ignatius of Antioch, an anonymous letter attributed to Barnabas, an apology to Diognetus, a homily (*2 Clement*), a manual of instruction (*Didache*), and collected visions and teachings (*Shepherd of Hermas*).

Social ethics generally permeate these works. The NT directive to seek God's kingdom seems particularly evident. In *2 Clement*, Christians are exhorted toward mutual love (9.6) and righteousness (11.7). In *Shepherd of Hermas*, those who seek the seal of baptism must first be clothed in the twelve virtues and bear their names (*Herm. Sim.* 9.14–16). Several authors encourage the giving of alms and charity. Polycarp insists that alms deliver the giver from death (10.2), while the *Didache* urges charity for all who ask (1.5).

More broadly, the Apostolic Fathers arises at a transitional moment as the church discards its Jewish roots for more Hellenistic moorings. Of primary concern is the question of what ethics might be for Christians as they separate from the customary moral doctrines of the synagogue.

The authors of *1 Clement* and the *Didache* take a conservative view, envisioning an ethic that continues to cling to conventional Jewish ideals. The letter of *1 Clement* is written to correct a situation at Corinth in which younger elders have removed the established leadership of the church without due process. The author responds by offering Moses as a model by which leaders should execute their duties. The unique nature of this Jewish prophet serves as a key to how all Christians must live. There is nothing more divine than to live in order and harmony as is befitting God's will in the manner of patience, humility, righteousness, and self-control. Though explicitly directed toward Corinth's leadership, such attributes surface throughout the work as essential for the life of the larger community.

The *Didache* embraces a parallel position, offering the Decalogue as a foundation for correct Christian living. Prohibitions against acts such as murder, adultery, and theft form the structure of a desirable community ideal. At the same time, the *Didache* integrates warnings against lesser transgressions in order to protect the faithful from even greater sins. Included here are cautions against worldly practices such as magic, sorcery, abortion, infanticide, astrology, and idolatry (1.1–6.2). These sins typify the "way of death" and find analogous warnings in *Barn.* 18–20. The *Didache* counsels Christians to walk in the "way of life" instead, attending to the wisdom that paves its path. The "two ways" is popular within late Judaism and Qumran (see 1QS 3.13–4.26), as well as elsewhere among early Christians (see *Herm. Mand.* 6.1–10).

Other authors in this literature depart notably from any vision of ethics that depends on traditional Jewish norms, instead typically integrating elements of Hellenistic philosophy and instruction. The letters of Ignatius and the *Epistle to Diognetus* best illustrate this view.

Ignatius, bishop of Antioch, writes seven letters to churches in Asia Minor and Italy as soldiers take him to martyrdom in Rome early in the second century. He fears unstable leadership, Christians who would return the church to Judaism, and the threat of Docetism. These concerns push him toward a three-tiered model of institutional leadership that features a central overseer (bishop) and a cadre of supporters (deacons and presbyters). Like *1 Clement* and *Hermas*, both from Rome, Ignatius speaks of endurance, unity, and patience. He envisions church harmony to be an express result of compliance with the will of the bishop. The duty of Christians is to model their lives around the directives of God's duly ordained leaders, who provide regulation through correct liturgical practice and appropriate theological confession. For Ignatius, an ethical lifestyle means an existence of obedience.

The *Epistle to Diognetus* takes a more Stoic approach to Christian ethics. After indicating the various ways in which Christianity is superior to the foolish worship practices of Jews and the idolatry of pagans, the author argues that Christians live in the world much like a soul dwells within a body. They reside on earth, unseen, suffering wrong, loving those who hate them, and existing as immortal beings, appointed by God for the benefit of the mortal world (6.1–10). It is because they are citizens of another kingdom that believers in Christ quietly suffer injustice, become poor, and experience dishonor and slander. This concept ultimately became a foundation for Augustine's *The City of God* and has influenced Christian views of ethics in the West.

Between these extremes are several authors who combine Jewish and Hellenistic themes in their understanding of what it means to live an ethical lifestyle. The bishop Polycarp, for instance, is concerned for order and harmony within the church, much like his contemporary Ignatius and the author of *1 Clement*. In contrast to the latter text, however, he hesitates to incorporate OT texts when arguing on behalf of righteousness as a key to being Christian. His warnings to avoid any temptation toward slander, greed, and false testimony (4.3) and his admonitions to be gentle, steadfast, and enduring in patience (12.2) largely reflect NT themes and ideals, which find distinctive parallel in the teachings of Ignatius. Polycarp may actually seek to avoid a close connection with Judaism because of open hostility between the synagogue and church in Smyrna. The author of the *Martyrdom of Polycarp* ultimately accuses the Jews there of instigating his death.

Two other authors run beyond Ignatius and Polycarp in the use of OT texts in detailing an ethical lifestyle, though they make use of these materials in differing ways. The author of *2 Clement* composes an entire homily based on Isa. 54. In reflection of the prophet's words, Christians are encouraged to endure their suffering in patience with the hope of God's future reward. They are warned to avoid adultery, slander, and jealousy; they are enticed to be self-controlled, merciful, and kind (4.2). As transients in the world, Christians must live a holy and righteous life in order to obtain God's kingdom.

The *Epistle of Barnabas*, however, once more lays claim to the figure of Moses as an ideal for those who would be faithful to God. Unlike *1 Clement*, this author uses the prophet as a counterbalance to the faithlessness of the early Israelites. Whereas Moses acted with distinction in revealing the divine will for the chosen people, the Jews ultimately forsook their right to this covenant with God through their disobedience to the demands of that agreement.

It is now for Christians to meet those same contractual demands in faith, thus to complete their true role as the people of God in a lifestyle of ethical piety. The ethical agenda of the Apostolic Fathers is both broad and inclusive, featuring the essentials of traditional Jewish values and incorporating the best of Hellenistic moral concerns. The mixture of these elements is inconsistent, however, hinting at the diverse ways in which early NT values would ultimately become fixed within later patristic ethical values.

Bibliography

Brändle, R. *Die Ethik der Schrift an Diognet: Eine Wiederaufnahme paulinischer und johanneischer Theologie am Ausgang des zweiten Jahrhunderts.* ATANT 64. Theologischer Verlag, 1975.

Holmes, M., ed. and trans. *The Apostolic Fathers: Greek Texts and English Transla-tions.* 3rd ed. Baker Academic, 2007.

Jefford, C. *The Apostolic Fathers and the New Testament.* Hendrickson, 2006, 73–106.

McDonald, J. *The Crucible of Christian Morality.* RFCC. Routledge, 1998.

◆ Didache ◆

Clayton N. Jefford

The *Teaching of the Twelve Apostles*, or the *Didache* (Gk. *didachē* ["teach-ing"]), is an early Christian manual of instruction whose origins remain un-known. Most scholars date the work to the late first or early second century, with a provenance somewhere between Egypt and Syria. Familiarity with limited themes from Paul and the sayings of Jesus, mainly as reflected in the Gospel of Matthew, is evident throughout. The text plausibly divides into three parts: the teaching of the "two ways" (chaps. 1–6), various liturgical and ecclesiastical instructions (chaps. 7–15), and concluding apocalyptic warnings (chap. 16).

Many Christians by the turn of the second century sought to create a new ethic with origins that lay outside of the synagogue. Against this tendency, the *Didache* appeals to those NT authors who endorse a functional ethic from within Judaism. Two primary elements from this more Jewish perspective appear here: a concern for eschatology and the "two ways."

The language of eschatology emerges randomly throughout the latter half of the work. One hears a call for the coming of God's kingdom and that heaven's work be done on earth, as illustrated by the Lord's Prayer (8.2). So too, supplication is offered for the ingathering of the church from the ends of the earth (9.4) and from the four winds (10.5). In light of the Lord's dominion, appropriate liturgical practices and good conduct in how peripatetic prophets are received are encouraged. A brief apocalyptic piece (chap. 16), reminiscent of Paul (1 Thess. 4:13–18) and Mark 13, concludes the text. Here the faithful of God are warned to be careful, to gather frequently, and to avoid false prophets as lawlessness increases before that day when the Lord comes from the skies with the sound of a trumpet. Typical of apocalyptic literature generally, this final warning intends for the listener to live ethically in the hope of eternal reward. It casts a shadow of urgency over the entire collection of teachings, much as Revelation does for the larger canon of Christian Scripture.

Apart from the broad community ethic associated with proper liturgical and ecclesiastical practice, the *Didache* is particularly interested in the question of individual ethics. This is evident in the opening line of the work: "There are two ways, one of life and one of death" (1.1). The "two ways" perspective developed from OT roots (Deut. 30:15; Jer. 21:8) into a common late Jewish directive (see *T. Ash.* 1.3–9; 1QS 3.13–4.26) whose branches extended into the NT (see Matt. 7:13–14). The Apostolic Fathers preserve this teaching in *Did.* 1–6, *Barn.* 18–20, and *Herm. Mand.* 6.1–10, revealing broad usage of this moral standard throughout the early second-century church. The "two ways" are often associated with angels of light and darkness in literature, though not so in the *Didache*.

The "way of life" in the *Didache* follows two principles. The first is the double command to love God and neighbor, thus directing the listener to-ward observance of the Shema (Deut. 6:4) coupled with a charge to respect other people (Lev. 19:18). This link is variously attributed to the teachings of Jesus elsewhere in the tradition (Matt. 22:37–40 pars.). Within broad rabbinic practice, to love God and neighbor is equivalent to satisfying the requirements of the Torah generally. To meet this essential requirement of God is to fulfill one's obligation to live righteously. The text also contains a negative form of the so-called Golden Rule to describe the appropriate treatment of neighbors: "Whatever you do not wish for yourself, do not do to another." Among the NT Gospels, only Matthew equates the double command and Golden Rule with "the law and the prophets" (Matt. 7:12; 22:40).

The second rule to which the Didachist turns for the essential framework of the "two ways" is the Decalogue. Here the author warns the listener to avoid murder and adultery, idolatry and theft, and the like. These sins are primary snares of the "way of death" (chap. 5). In similar fashion, the *Didache* lists prohibitions against practicing worldly sins, such as magic, sorcery, abor-tion, hypocrisy, arrogance, astrology, and so forth. Such transgressions are stepping-stones to greater sins. Following rabbinic technique, the Didachist cautions against these lesser indiscretions in order to erect a fence around the more vital teaching of the Decalogue itself. Here the listener discerns an early Jewish-Christian argument for the need to respect the teachings of Torah and to practice an ethic pleasing to both God and humanity.

Secondarily inserted into the "two ways" segment are injunctions from the early church known as the "ecclesiastical interpolation" (1.3b–2.1a). Included here are instructions to bless, pray, and fast for one's enemies, to love one's opponents, to resist aggression, and to give gladly and not receive. Parallel teachings appear in the sermon materials of Matt. 5:38–48 and Luke 6:27–36, which may be the source for these sayings in the *Didache*. The presence of this insertion suggests that the *Didache* reflects an evolving community ethic. It is built on an early Jewish foundation featuring eschatological promise and warning, a "two ways" directive of the Shema and a command to love one's neighbor, an exposition of the Decalogue with a defensive hedge against secondary offenses, and the late addition of Jesus' teachings on the nature of sacrificial love. The agenda is expressly Jewish in form, though essentially Christian in flavor.

The *Didache* was widely known among later patristic writers, most of whom abandoned the shape of its ethics, undoubtedly because of the author's emphasis on a decidedly Jewish perspective.

Bibliography

Balabanski, V. *Eschatology in the Making: Matthew, Mark, and the Didache*. SNTSMS 97. Cambridge University Press, 1997, 180–209.

Kloppenborg, J. "The Transformation of Moral Exhortation in *Didache* 1–5." Pages 88–109 in *The Didache in Context: Essays on Its Text, History, and Transmission*, ed. C. Jefford. NovTSup 77. Brill, 1995.

Osborn, E. "The Love Command in Second Century Christian Writing." *SecCent* 1 (1981): 223–43.

Rordorf, W. "An Aspect of the Judeo-Christian Ethic: The Two Ways." Pages 148–64 in *The Didache in Modern Research*, ed. J. Draper. AGJU 37. Brill, 1996.

INDEX OF SCRIPTURE AND ANCIENT WRITINGS

INDEX OF SUBJECTS

Printed and bound by CPI Group (UK) Ltd, Croydon, CR0 4YY

13/04/2025

14656459-0005